1001 Great Ideas

for Teaching and Raising Children with Autism Spectrum Disorders

"Destined to become a staple for those who love, live or work with children with autism. The authors' voices are authoritative and comforting. Perhaps most importantly, they are spot on with the issues. A toolkit packed with ideas, resources, suggestions, and a good dose of encouragement, validation and yes: redemption."
Jennifer McCammon, Publisher, Portland Family Magazine

"A friendly voice offering parents and teachers immediately usable ideas that emphasize the practical rather than the technical. Well organized for quick reading, with major ideas preceded by helpful introductory text. A great resource that parents and teachers should keep readily available."
Christine Hunt, MS, special education and resource teacher

"*1001 Great Ideas* goes beyond a list of things to do with your child who has autism. The thoughtful comments about why these suggestions are purposeful and valuable as teaching tools make this a *must have* for families, childcare providers and special education professionals. The insights the authors share throughout the book put the activities into a real life focus for working with children on the autism spectrum."
Nancy Seller, Ed.S., Education Division Director

"Great book—couldn't put it down. So many creative ideas, and all of them detailed and easy to follow. I like reaching children through fun, so I appreciated the suggestions for games, activities and specific reading titles that we can go right to. The IEP suggestions are helpful for both parents and school staff, the authors' sidenotes about their own experiences are insightful."
Karla Mayer, MS, CCC-SLP

"*1001 Great Ideas* is just that, a treasure trove of wonderful ideas and activities! This hope-filled book not only connects the reader to the world of Autism Spectrum Disorders but also provides a multitude of practical solutions to the broad range of challenges that parents and professional face each and every day. *1001 Great Ideas* is a resource that both parents and professionals will continually turn to."
Scott Tanner, School Psychologist & Director of Clinical Services

1001 Great Ideas

for Teaching and Raising Children with Autism Spectrum Disorders

By Ellen Notbohm and Veronica Zysk

Future Horizons, Inc.

1001 Great Ideas

All marketing and publishing rights guaranteed to and reserved by

721 W. Abram Street
Arlington, Texas 76013
800-489-0727
817-277-0727
817-277-2270 (fax)
E-mail: info@FHautism.com
www.FHautism.com

The information presented in this book is educational and should not be construed as offering diagnostic, treatment or legal advice or consultation. If professional assistance in any of these areas is needed, the services of a competent autism professional should be sought.

ISBN 1-932565-19-1

Contents

Preface

Whether or not you believe in fate, karma or serendipity, there was an impetus greater than mere coincidence that brought the two of us authors together. Veronica had been an autism professional for many years, the head of a national autism organization, an administrative VP for our publisher, Future Horizons, a book editor and now spends her days as managing editor of the *Autism Asperger's Digest*—the first national magazine released on autism spectrum disorders. All these things—but not a parent. All the way on the other side of the continent, Ellen had been the parent of a son with autism for exactly as many years, a freelance writer and communications consultant—but with no professional autism credentials at all. Forces were set in motion when Ellen submitted an article about her son's tussles with literacy to the *Digest*. Over the course of the ensuing year or so, conversation after conversation ended up in the same place: our vastly different experiences dovetailed quite beautifully to form a remarkable partnership—but to what end? That was yet unrevealed to us. Our experiences alone would not have been magnetic enough to foster collaboration on a project the magnitude of this one. What unfolded and became compelling was a set of mutually held beliefs and values about the autism condition. These were forces that bound us together, soul to soul. Collaborative ideas got kicked around for months, and then came the opportunity to write this book together.

Those beliefs and values pervade our writing, and you won't be able to miss them because they distill down to three deceptively simple—but enormously intricate—elements.

At the very core of our discourse is sensory integration. Veronica is able to make Ellen go crazy every time she tells her that there are still folks in the field of autism who view sensory integration therapy as an as-time-allows add-on to "real" treatments. Or, that she hears from parents who regard it as unscientific hogwash, or teachers who never, ever incorporate it into their classroom strategy. Is it because the topic is so intensely complex that many parents and even professionals simply turn away from it, hoping for an easier solution? Such an attitude is certainly understandable. Neurology is a very, very complicated proposition. Katharine Hepburn in *The African Queen* provides us with the definitive approach. When the German officer protests that her journey down an unnavigable river is impossible, her response is: "Never. The. Less."

Never in your parenting or teaching experience will it be more important to do whatever is necessary to put yourself in the shoes—in the skin—of another, especially one whose sensory systems are inexplicably wired differently. The child who is experiencing hyper-acute sensory responses to his world is in a state of constant self-defense against an environment that is spinning, shrieking, squeezing and otherwise assaulting him incessantly. To expect social or cognitive learning to take place under such conditions is simply counter-intuitive to us, thus we place major emphasis on sensory integration. You'll see it throughout the book—in just the same manner that sensory inputs pervade real life for not just children with ASD, but for all of us. Sensory therapy must be the cornerstone of any treatment program for this population. We know this because we've seen it up close. As a preschooler, Ellen's son exhibited extreme tactile, oral, aural, visual and proprioceptive defensiveness. After seven years of focused sensory intervention, he was dismissed from both occupational therapy and adapted PE programs because his skills and sensitivities in these areas were no longer distinguishable from his neuro-typical peers. It wasn't magic. It was sensory intervention. Sustained, patient sensory intervention.

Shoulder-to-shoulder with sensory intervention is the significance we place on communication and language therapy. There simply can't be any argument that a child who cannot make his needs known and thereby met is going to be a simmering cauldron of frustration and despair. Research tells us that 40% of our children with ASD are nonverbal, that a majority of these children will never develop functional language. We just don't agree, and that incites us to be vocal with parents and professionals about the importance of giving children—all children—on the spectrum a means to communication. Whether it's through sign language, a picture system, or verbal language doesn't really matter; that they have a communication system does. Try to imagine yourself going through your day unable to keep pace, comprehend or contribute to the conversation around you, not possessing the means or the vocabulary to tell your boss or mate that you hurt or need or want, being unable to decode the symbols on a page or the sounds coming out of a telephone. As with sensory integration, the day becomes a minute-to-minute struggle to merely cope; no true learning can take place in such an environment. "If the English language made any sense, a catastrophe would be an apostrophe with fur," Doug Larson tells us. Any speech therapist or English Language Learner teacher will tell you that English is arguably the most treacherous language on the planet. For concrete thinkers like our kids with ASD, the English language with its inconsistent rules, abstract idioms, nuances of sarcasm, homophones, multiple meaning words and seemingly nonsensical words like "pineapple" (which contains neither pine nor apple) is a desperate morass. Early, intense and ongoing language/communication therapy is crucial, and happily, it is an area where a little awareness enables adults to make a difference at every hour of the day. We've included lots of ideas in this area so you can do just that.

Overreaching all of this is our most heartfelt conviction that the ultimate power to live with and overcome autism lies in our unfettered willingness to love the child or student with ASD *absolutely unconditionally*. Only when we are free of "what-if?" and "if he would just," will we have a child who himself is free to bloom within his own abilities (he has many), his own personality, his own timeline (not ours or what is "developmentally appropriate"). It is no less than you wanted for yourself as a child, and it is no less than what you want for yourself as an adult. Yes, Virginia, there *is* a magic bullet. A child who feels unconditional acceptance and perceives that the significant adults around him truly believe that "he can do it" has every chance of becoming the happy, competent adult we always hoped and dreamed he would be.

A friend of Ellen's asked about the title of the book, *1001 Great Ideas*. Didn't it seem a little overwhelming? Well, Ellen replied without really thinking, it has a sort of Scheherazade quality to it that I like.

Her friend was speechless. Where did that come from?

The truth is, it came out of nowhere, but under analysis, it became quite apt. In the tale popularly known as *1001 Arabian Nights*, the king of an unnamed island has been so angered by his wife's infidelity that he kills her, then gives an order that a new wife come to him each night. At the end of each night he kills her too. When Scheherazade appears before the king for the first time, she begins to tell him a tale that ends in a cliff-hanger. The king's curiosity is piqued just enough that he doesn't kill her but instead has her back the next night—and the next, and the next, and each night the story has just enough suspense to merit its continuation. At the end of 1001 nights, the king has long since given up the thought of killing his now-beloved companion.

Scheherazade stayed alive because each day ended with her creating in the king an inquisitiveness, a wanting to know what events, what insights, what possibilities the next day held. Autism is such an experience, if you will let it be so. Each day you stay alive is another day understanding it, integrating it, embracing its presence and its gifts (yes) as part of your life. Use that curiosity to stir in yourself the courage to get up and try one more time, the stamina to forge on when it's appropriate and the wisdom to know when to walk away and fight another day, the perspective to move on to Plan B when Plan A isn't working.

The gift of a rich and meaningful life for you and your child with autism awaits you.

Acknowledgements

Any book that accepts the challenge of putting forth 1001 ideas (all of them good, of course) would of necessity have to be an ensemble piece. We are gratefully indebted each and every day to the community of outstanding individuals who have enhanced our lives, and now our book, with their expertise, their can-do (actually, *will*-do) attitude and their devotion to children with autism and the broader world we all share. Through this book, we are but funnels for their collective wisdom and years of effort on behalf of children like the author's son and countless other children with ASD and other supplemental needs.

Unhappy it is that Greg Jones, principal extraordinaire at Capitol Hill Elementary School in Portland, Oregon cannot be bottled and sold. An outstanding school like Capitol Hill, one that opens its arms and heart to supplemental needs children, is a tops-down proposition; come see for yourself. Resource teachers and therapists like Mary Schunk and Julianne Barker are beyond the reach of superlatives. The fingerprints of Nola Shirley, Lucy Courtney, Diane Larson, Sharon Martine, Marcia Wirsig, Jackie Druck, Terry Clifford and Annie Westfall are all over this book as well.

No one should undertake the journey through autism without an occupational therapist like Veda Nomura. If you do not have a Veda, for heaven's sake, go get one at once. A bottomless pit of passion for her work and patience for her clients, she may be the largest single contributor to this book and certainly to broadening our understanding of autism.

Sarah Spella, Robin Jensen, Jean Motley, Arielle Bernstein, Lori Heimbichner, Emily Polanshek and Lacee Jones contributed brilliant ideas from their own experiences and jogged ones we had forgotten.

We send heartfelt thanks to the many autism professionals whose work awakened in us reservoirs of ideas that we didn't even know existed in us. Thanks go out to Temple Grandin, David Freschi, and Reed Martin for sharing their knowledge and expertise in ways they might not even have imagined.

A special thanks to our publisher and friend, Wayne Gilpin. Always the visionary, his Don Quixote approach to publishing is a guiding light to authors, like ourselves, in making our dreams a reality.

To our adored parents, whether they are with us in body or in spirit, your presence is the safe haven that gives us courage to venture forth and discover the adventures that lie beyond the edge of our comfort zone. Your influence is felt daily and only intensifies as time passes.

The "significant others" in our lives—be they husbands or friends—have been unfailingly supportive of our efforts to produce this book. There is a squirm factor in putting your own experiences and mistakes under a microscope, and they've been there for us as cheerleaders, confidants, sounding boards and critics. You render us speechless—we who are wordsmiths—in expressing how important you are to us.

We celebrate every person with ASD who has entered our lives, furthering our understanding and our appreciation of their courage, their unique abilities and their individuality. But in the end, there are no individuals more responsible for shaping us (sometimes under protest) and our ability to write this book than Connor and Bryce. Whatever cosmology underwrote sending you to us, it is an honor for which we'll feel always and endlessly grateful.

Ellen Notbohm
Veronica Zysk
September 2004

Glossary

ABA	Applied Behavioral Analysis
ADA	American with Disabilities Act
Antecedent	A cue, trigger, impetus, incident or person that immediately precedes a behavior. Think of it as the "if" portion of an "if-then" proposition—a condition that comes before an event.
ASD	Autism Spectrum Disorder
Bilateral activity	In this book, we refer to bilateral activity as physical activity that utilizes both sides of the body equally, such as swimming, biking, jumping rope, running.
Consequence	An outcome or effect that conditionally follows a behavior. Think of it as the "then" portion of an "if-then" proposition. (*See Antecedent*)
Echolalia/echolalic	Rote repetition of the conversation of others (immediate echolalia) or of scripts or past conversations (delayed echolalia). May be functional, as in repeating a line from a movie within a relevant situation, may be used as a self-stimulant (calming) device, or may be involuntary and accompanied by little or no comprehension.
Functional Behavior Analysis (FBA)	Procedure for determining the root or cause of a behavior before developing an interceptive course of action. Under IDEA, schools must complete an FBA when addressing problem behaviors, although specific guidelines for the administration of the FBA are not spelled out under the law.

Hyper-sensitivity   Occurs when a person's auditory, visual, tactile and other senses are overly acute, causing painful responses to "normal" stimuli.

Hypo-sensitivity   Occurs when a person's auditory, visual, tactile and other senses are under-responsive, giving the brain little to no information with which to interpret and respond to environment.

IDEA   Individuals with Disabilities Education Act. Provides federal funding to state and local education systems to facilitate meeting the needs of students with disabilities. In accepting the funding, states and school systems are bound by the Act's substantive and procedural mandates. Ensures access to free and appropriate education for children with disabilities through both administrative and judicial avenues.

NT   "Neuro-typical," a person who does not have an autism spectrum disorder

OT   Occupational therapist, a specialist trained in developing interventions, treatments and activities addressing hyper- or hypo-acute responses to a child's fine motor skills, visual perceptual skills, sensory motor skills, life skills, pre-vocational skills, social/emotional development and functional mobility.

Perseveration/ Perseverative behavior/Perseverate   A form of "persevere," perseveration is the continuation of a response or a behavior long beyond the original impetus.

Positive reinforcement   An action, item or words that increase the likelihood that desired behavior will be repeated; a reward.

Proprioception — The ability to sense the position, location, orientation and movement of the body and its parts.

Punishment — Penalty or adverse consequence imposed in response to undesirable behavior.

Reinforcer — An object, token, stimulus or other result that supports or encourages the recurrence or continuation of the behavior immediately preceding.

Section 504 — Section 504 is a clause in the Rehabilitation Act of 1973 requiring that, "no otherwise qualified handicapped individual shall, solely by reason of her or his disability, be excluded from participation in, be denied the benefits of, or be subjected to discrimination under any program or activity receiving federal financial assistance." Under this Federal law, schools are prohibited from discriminating against students with disabilities.

Self-regulation — Routines, techniques, tactics or strategies that help a child manage his or her own behavior and thoughts throughout various settings and changes in environment.

Sensory Integration (SI) — Ability to use information from all seven senses to manage daily activity and communicate with others. The seven senses are: tactile (touch), olfactory (smell), auditory (hearing), visual (sight), gustatory (taste), vestibular (equilibrium/gravity) and proprioceptive (body position awareness).

SLP — Speech/Language Pathologist

Social Stories

A Social Story is a short story—defined by specific characteristics—that describes a situation, concept, or social skill. It is a carefully scripted text that describes a *process* and a *result* in terms that make sense and are applicable to the person with ASD.

Stimulus

An input, cue, action, influence or anything that evokes a response.

Theory of Mind (ToM)

The ability to understand that others have beliefs, desires and intentions that are different from one's own.

Token system

A behavior reinforcement system wherein the child earns tokens or markers for achieving desired behaviors. Upon accumulating an agreed-upon number of tokens, he can exchange them for pre-determined reward activities or items.

Vestibular

The sense that regulates our equilibrium. Vestibular means relating to the vestibule of the ear, an opening at the inner ear that contains the saccule and utricle—the organs of equilibrium. This system regulates our body movement through space, synchronizes movements of the head and body and is closely connected to the auditory and visual senses. Vestibular disorder can manifest in "gravitational insecurity," a frightening sense of falling when the position of the head changes.

Chapter 1

The Radar-Net of Our Senses

Sensory Integration Strategies and Considerations

There is no way in which to understand the world without first detecting it through the radar-net of our senses.

Diane Ackerman

Sensory motor activities you can do at home. Of all the baffling aspects of autism, perhaps none is more baffling to the lay person than sensory integration. Through a complex series of atypical signals/connections in the brain, the child with ASD experiences sights, sounds, touches, smells, tastes and gravity in a manner profoundly different from that of typical children and adults. Every minute of their daily life may be a battle against invasive sensations that overwhelm their hyper-acute sensory systems. Or conversely, their senses may be hypo-active, requiring major effort to alert their bodies so that learning can take place. Layered on top of that may be an inability to process more than one sensory modality at a time.

Step for a moment inside the body of a child with sensory integration difficulties in this excerpt from the author's article, "What Every Child with Autism Wishes You Knew" (Child's Voice, Children's Welfare League of America, November 2004):

> "My sensory perceptions are disordered. This means that the ordinary sights, sounds, smells, tastes and touches of everyday that you may not even notice can be downright painful for me. The very environment in which I have to live often seems hostile. I may appear withdrawn or belligerent to you but I am really just trying to defend myself. Here is why a "simple" trip to the grocery store may be hell for me:
>
> My hearing may be hyper-acute. Dozens of people are talking at once. The loud speaker booms today's special. Musak whines from the sound system. Cash registers beep and cough, a coffee grinder is chugging. The meat cutter screeches, babies wail, carts creak, the fluorescent lighting hums. My brain can't filter all the input and I'm in overload!
>
> My sense of smell may be highly sensitive. The fish at the meat counter isn't quite fresh, the guy standing next to us hasn't showered today, the deli is handing out sausage samples, the baby in line ahead of us has a poopy diaper, they're mopping up pickles on aisle 3 with ammonia—I can't sort it all out; I'm too nauseous.

Because I am visually oriented [see more on this below], this may be my first sense to become overstimulated. The fluorescent light is too bright; it makes the room pulsate and hurts my eyes. Sometimes the pulsating light bounces off everything and distorts what I am seeing— the space seems to be constantly changing. There's glare from windows, too many items for me to be able to focus (I may compensate with "tunnel vision"), moving fans on the ceiling, so many bodies in constant motion. All this affects my vestibular sense, and now I can't even tell where my body is in space."

When we take all this into consideration, it becomes easy to see how many so-called inappropriate behaviors are rooted in sensory defensiveness. Believe—*really believe*—that no child wants the negative or punitive feedback they get from "bad" behavior. Calming or alerting over- or under-active senses will go a very long way toward helping the child master socially acceptable behavior. This very achievable and worthwhile process requires patience and consistency, so start slowly and stay the course. What seems impossibly incremental *is* working.

We're starting you off with many easy and useful ideas for different ways to incorporate sensory activities into your child's day. Some of the ideas are appropriate for both home and school; all are designed to get you thinking beyond the traditional activities that might easily come to mind. And remember, while sensory activities provide important clues to your child's brain about the world around him and can aid in desensitizing the child to sensory difficulties, they can be fun-filled, too. Be playful; kids love it. No less an authority than Dr. Seuss said, "Have you ever flown a kite in bed? Have you ever walked with ten cats on your head? If you never have, you should. These things are fun and fun is good" (*One Fish, Two Fish, Red Fish, Blue Fish,* Random House, 1960).

Finger painting. Ah, the lovely, slippery, squishy feel of paint on fingers and palms—most of us fondly recall this favorite childhood activity—a chance to really get our hands messy in an appropriate way. All that good "sensory feel" might not feel so good to some of our ASD kids. So, keep it interesting and fun with substances that differ in texture and viscosity:

- Paint
- Shaving Cream
- Pudding
- Colored bath gel

And, think beyond fingers: paint in these substances with feet or toes or even elbows.

Sand table. Sand provides great resistance for proprioceptive input, but it's really just the beginning. Try some of these alternatives to fill the sand table:

- Rice (try it colored with a few drops of food coloring for added interest)
- Beans/lentils
- Kitty litter (hint: the kind made from ground nut shells or corn)
- Potting soil or dirt
- Popcorn (unpopped or popped)
- Birdseed
- Oatmeal
- Home aquarium rocks
- Pea gravel

Sand table activities. There's more to a sand table than just scooping sand, filling buckets and dumping it out again. These simple activities provide important sensory and motor development in eye-hand coordination, vestibular input and proprioception. They carry the added benefit of providing opportunities to teach opposite concepts, such as "in/out", "here/there" or "full/empty." Help children explore the terrain through activities that require them to push/pull/drag/dig, giving them that all-important sensory feedback on a repeated basis:

- Digging for hidden objects
- Combine with water play, especially to change the texture of the material. Light and flaky oatmeal becomes thick and sticky in spots with water added to it. Splashing the water into the oatmeal becomes part of the fun.
- Play with action figures: They can march, exercise, snuggle, move on their tummies, jump—whatever keeps them moving through the substance.
- Play with construction vehicles: making hills, roads, digging holes.

Rolling. We mean the whole-body kind that can be a source of delight and laughter. Encourage your child to roll up or down or across different textures. Watch for signs of dizziness, nausea or disorientation—warning signs that sensory activity is too intense — and be ready to stop immediately.

- Grass: Roll on level ground or down a hill; then crawl back up the hill on his tummy.
- Carpet: thick and plush, sisal or indoor/outdoor
- Roll while inside a blanket: wool, cotton, thin or thick
- Roll while inside a large box (cut off top and bottom to form a tube)

Simon-Says games. Any game where kids imitate can be a rich environment for incorporating sensory integration experiences. Simon Says, Follow the Leader or obstacle courses all incorporate fun, gross motor body movements that supply constant sensory information to the child's brain. Get their whole bodies involved in:

- Crawling
- Jumping (especially in patterns)
- Hopping (two feet, one foot, holding one foot, arms overhead with hands clasped together)
- Running (forwards, backwards, sideways, in circles)

- Wiggling or slithering (have them try it without using their hands or arms)
- Rolling

Your Follow-the-Leader path can take the child through various sensory areas in and out of your house—carpet, patio, wading pool, sandbox, etc. Pretend you are various different animals, sometimes walking on two feet, sometimes four, flying, "dry" swimming, meowing, cawing and roaring as appropriate.

> *Tip:* While silly can be fun and silly is okay, some very literal-thinking kids with autism won't appreciate your silliness, at least at first. Be prepared to modify activities to suit their interest and learning styles. Remember to keep an eye out for sensory overload and know when to shift into a calming activity.

Food fun. Perhaps your little one doesn't like to get his hands dirty, but helping you make a snack or part of dinner would be an acceptable way to experience tactile sensations. Try these ideas instead:

- Mixing/patting/rolling out cookie dough by hand
- Mixing guacamole by hand, including mashing the avocado with fingers first
- Mixing meatloaf by hand, including squishing those eggs; cold hamburger right out of the 'fridge adds another level of input
- Beating pudding or pancake batter with a rotary beater
- Mixing cake batter by hand with a whisk
- Churning butter in a jar until it firms up
- Creating cookie shapes in dough with cookie cutters or with a cookie press
- Kneading bread dough
- Making figures out of marshmallows or gum drops; joined by pretzel sticks or toothpicks

Gross motor input. Lots of kids with ASD benefit from "heavy work" where they need to really move their muscles against resistance in order for signals to reach their brain. Chores around the house are perfect for this type of vestibular and proprioceptive input, with the added bonus that your child can take pride in being part of the family structure and helping out.

- Carrying/dragging the laundry basket
- Pushing the lawn mower (use discretion)
- Pushing the grocery cart at the store
- Pushing the vacuum cleaner
- Carrying groceries in from the car
- Digging in the garden with a shovel or trowel
- Hammering
- Pulling a wagon or pushing a wheelbarrow
- Pumping up the beach ball or inner tube with a foot or hand pump; ditto with bicycle tire pumps
- Mop or sweep floors or the patio, or dirt
- Take turns pulling a sibling on a sheet or blanket "sled"
- Pull a wheeled suitcase (full)
- Dragging that twenty-five-pound bag of bird seed to the feeder and then filling it up

Swinging or spinning. Many ASD kids love to spin. Right along with spinning is swinging. OTs and SLPs frequently work together as they've found that language often emerges while ASD kids are swinging or involved in some fun large movement activity. Be creative with swinging and spinning:

- **Swing** in a regular playground-type swing, a hammock or net swing, or a tire swing
- Try a platform swing (usually carpet- or foam-covered plywood sheet)
- A pipe/bolster swing (large fabric covered capped plastic pipe) that they can lie over stomach-down

- A trapeze
- **Spin** using any of the above equipment
- Spin in place: arms at sides/arms outstretched/arms overhead
- Spin in the pool or the shallow part of a lake
- Spin in the rain—standing in a puddle
- Spin with another person, arms outstretched with hands touching at each spin, like gears working together; how fast can you both go and still touch at each spin?

Fine motor activities. While gross motor activities can rev your child up when he's lethargic or calm him down when stress and anxiety are present, fine motor activities are useful in helping him better navigate his day-to-day world. For the child whose fine motor skills are challenged, eating, dressing, writing, doing homework, grooming—all can be difficult to some extent or another. Start early on in their lives providing lots of fine motor activities for your child to allow his or her sensory systems to make the connection between touch and function.

- Drawing or writing with a battery-operated vibrating pen: especially helpful for kids whose sense of touch is sensitive.
- Drawing or writing with chalk (use an easel, a sidewalk, or slate)
- Use different textured items to erase the chalk—eraser, dishcloth, fingers, elbows, paper napkin, etc.
- Use a finger to write a letter on each other's back, tummy or back of hand and try to guess each one without looking
- Use a pencil to "write" in Play-doh® or clay
- Hang a piece of metal sheeting (cover sharp edges and fold back) as a magnet board for letters, shapes, characters, etc.
- Puppet play—finger puppets, hand puppets, shadow puppets
- Playing with glue—spreading it around the paper with a finger or a Q-tip®
- Playing with wind-up toys

- Stringing beads, curtain rings, pretzel twists, buttons, etc; popcorn or cranberries for holidays or for your feathered friends anytime
- Etch-a-sketch

Bathroom sensory inputs. Bath time is another everyday activity that can provide all sorts of sensory feedback to your child's system. Capitalize on the opportunity whenever possible.

- After the bath or shower, brisk towel drying with lots of pressure
- Rubbing body lotion on his or her arms and legs
- Brushing teeth with a battery-operated toothbrush

Water, water everywhere (they wish!) Many children on the spectrum are fond of any kind of water play. Water activities are filled with different textures, temperatures and smells, providing all sorts of different sensory input. That may be good or not-so-good, depending on your child. Stay attuned to certain aspects that might interfere with the overall experience and make it less than appealing.

- Washing dishes, especially in soapy water up to his elbow
- Playing in mud: thick and oozy or thinner and grainy
- Filling water cans and watering garden flowers
- Playing in puddles—stomping (especially with bare feet!), stirring with a stick, tossing pebbles in
- Washing the car or bike or dog with bucket or hose
- Water wiggle
- Floating on a raft or inner tube (perfect for more spinning!)
- Diving for objects (weighted rings, coins)

Blowin' in the wind. The articulator muscles around the mouth contribute to many tasks that are necessary to a child's over-all growth. Eating, speaking, singing, crying—even breathing and holding the head erect—all involve oral-motor development. For a child with low oral-motor tone, these everyday activities do not come easily.

Sucking and blowing are two excellent exercises that strengthen the articulator muscles. To follow are some ideas on each; the variations are endless.

Sucking. Sucking foods with a puree consistency through a straw will give the mouth a workout. Try pudding, pureed fruit (apple, pear, banana, strawberry, peach, melon), thick milkshakes or fruit smoothies, warm pureed soups like tomato, lentil or black bean, baby food desserts, yogurt (no fruit chunks), half-melted ice cream, sherbet, or sorbet, half-congealed Jello.

Using an ordinary drinking straw to suck these foods through is fine, but there are lots of fun alternatives. "Crazy straws" with twists and curves increase the sucking challenge. Pliable vinyl tubing comes in different widths and can be loosely tied into shapes, or simply left as is. Cocktail straws with their tiny opening require a different sucking motion and are fun for thinner liquids.

Blowing and puffing. Your child will probably love this rare opportunity to play with his food. Have her try to blow bubbles through the straw into a liquid or puree. Note together how the different substances react: root beer may work up a head, pudding looks like lava. Notice, too, how the scent of the food is released by the bubbles.

Get creative with blowing objects other than food. We know one child who liked to play Babe the Pig with a straw and a handful of cotton balls. The cotton balls were the sheep and the child was Babe, winning the sheepdog competition by blowing the sheep into formation. Another child built a log jam by blowing toilet tissue tubes "downriver," then piling then up and blowing them over. Any lightweight item will do for starters: wadded-up plastic wrap, ping-pong balls, feathers, cake-type ice cream cones, inflated balloons. Items and activities can increase in weight and difficulty as the child's oral musculature improves, e.g., a dried pinecone instead of a ping-pong ball, or trying to keep the balloon aloft rather than just blowing it across the floor. More advanced: blowing up the balloons herself, blowing bubbles with bubble gum. Some of the harder types of bubble gum that start as a ball get his jaw really moving just getting the gum pliable enough to blow the first bubble.

> *Tip:* Once your child has mastered the skill of blowing up a balloon, it can be a great stress dissipater. Have her blow her anger, frustration, anxiety or sillies into the balloon and pinch it shut but don't tie it off. Then have her hold it aloft and let go, blowing away her troubles as the balloon zooms around the room in a burst of (ahem) fart-like noise that most children find hilarious.

Fun with bubbles. Bubbles are a great sensory item. Here are some offbeat ways to go beyond pulling the same old wand out of the bottle.

- Make popping them a bilateral activity: Swing a fly swatter to produce the bubbles and then attack them, alternating hands. Or, pop them by clapping.
- Soap in the eyes can be painful. Make your own non-irritating bubble liquid by mixing 1/4 cup no-tears baby shampoo, 3/4 cup water, 3 tablespoons light corn syrup.
- Use cookie cutters to make bubbles in a shape that interests your child. Numbers, animals, Halloween items, stars.
- Try bubble blowing in the winter. What does a freezy bubble look like? (It will be colorless, unlike the purple tinge they have in summer.)
- Blow bubbles into a jar and try to get the lid on, trapping them. How long do they last?
- Wet your hands and try to catch and hold a bubble—contact with something dry is what causes them to pop. Try to move the bubble to your other hand.
- Blow bubbles through the Musical Bubble Clown (available from Magical Toys and Products), and hear a musical tune. www.magicaltoysandproducts.com

Not quite Willie Wonka but close. Clay and play dough are great sensory experiences, unless you spend the time taking your child's hand away from her mouth as she tries to eat the stuff. Make her day—with edible clay.

Recipe #1: Combine 1 cup powdered milk, 1/2 cup creamy peanut butter, 1/2 cup honey. Spray your child's hand with non-stick cooking spray and set her loose. She can eat the shapes she makes now or refrigerate for later.

Recipe #2: Combine 3 1/2 cups creamy peanut butter, 4 cups powdered sugar, 3 1/2 cups light corn syrup, 4 cups powdered milk.

> *Note: Do not use these recipes if your child is allergic to peanuts! (Recipes adapted from* www.surprisingkids.com*)*

Bits of sun. Here's a creative way to help little ones develop their fine motor skills. Give them a giant sunflower and tweezers to pick out the seeds. Use the seeds for crafts, art, counting or dry 'em and eat 'em.

Contact sports, kiddie-style. All of those fun kid-contact games your parents or grandparents played with you offer great tactile, vestibular and proprioceptive inputs. Time to bring these back, and aren't they a great way to get Dad involved? (Remember to monitor intensity carefully.)

- Horsey ride
- Piggyback ride
- Airplane ride
- Row, row, row your boat
- Trotting off to Boston
- This is the Way the Ladies Go

How does your engine run? The Alert Program helps students understand the basic theory of sensory integration. It uses the analogy of an automobile engine to introduce its concepts of self-regulation to students. "If your body is like a car engine, sometimes it runs on high, sometimes it runs on low, and sometimes it runs just right." Alert Program leaders work in three stages, helping children identify their engine speeds, experiment with methods to change engine speeds, and regulate their engine speeds. Kids master how to change their engine levels for a variety of settings, so they can do what they want to do (learn, work, play) in the arousal state appropriate for that task.

For more information on the Alert Program, contact TherapyWorks in New Mexico; www.AlertProgram.com. Many occupational therapists (OTs) are familiar with the Alert Program. If you're a parent, band together with a few other parents and ask your OT for a mini-inservice, so you know how to use the program at home, too.

Volume control. You know the signs: your child hurries to cover his ears when he hears certain sounds, easily gets agitated when the dishwasher or the neighbor's leaf blower is running, or will absolutely, positively never return to that one restaurant because it's right next door to the fire station, where the fire alarm went off five minutes into your last meal there. Sound sensitivities can wreak havoc in the lives of kids with ASD, be a constant source of anxiety, and cause discomfort or physical pain in some kids. Try a desensitizing program for the offending sound. Tape record the sound. Gradually introduce the sound to the child, starting with it at a very low volume. Allow the child to initiate the sound at gradually increasing volume. His or her control of the sound is a big part of the process, so go slowly at first until the child's confidence in handling the sound increases.

Things that go bump in the night. Going to sleep, especially in a place other than home, can be hard if hyper-sensitive ears pick up all those sounds that typical people push into the background and easily disregard. The uncertainty of not knowing when and how often an unfamiliar sound might arise, especially one that might be painful, can be a source of constant anxiety for these children.

Talk with your child about what kinds of sounds he might hear at night in another house or hotel. For some kids, making a game of listening to and identifying sounds might lessen the anxious feelings. Before he goes to bed, listen for: traffic noise such as sirens, buses or trains, footsteps or voices in the hall or overhead, various plumbing noises, crickets, birds, dogs or other animal sounds, elevators whooshing up and down, food carts rattling up the hall, sounds from an ice machine or other vending machines. Just knowing what the sounds are and that they are okay can help a child relax.

> *Tip*: When booking a hotel room, tell them you are traveling with a special needs child and request a room in a quiet area. That is, not near the elevator or over the kitchen, away from the main avenue or street, and not booked onto the floor with the all-night wedding or sports celebration going on.

Figure-ground processing. If your child seems tuned in to what children across the room are talking about, but is unaware of instructions being spoken directly to her, she may have difficulty with "figure-ground processing." This means she cannot distinguish between foreground and background noise. On a visual level, she may have trouble identifying the primary object in a picture from its surroundings. Figure-ground dysfunction can also translate into diminished sense of danger, exemplified by behaviors such as failing to stop before crossing the street or jumping from unsafe heights. Talk with your OT if you suspect your child has difficulties in this area.

Tactile helper. For the child who needs constant tactile input to help him stay on task, stay calm or self-regulate his sensory levels, use Velcro® to attach a surgical brush or other textured item (piece of fur, sandpaper) to the bottom of his desk.

Headphones, pro and con. Headphones may help shut out distractions for children with noise sensitivity, in a socially acceptable manner. Keep in mind that sounds not easily heard by others may be troublesome for a child on the spectrum. What we consider a "normal" amount of noise may be highly disturbing for these kids. But also be aware that having an object wrapped around their head may be worse than the noise for certain children. Moreover, there's research to suggest that repeated use of headphones can impair the child's hearing. Acclimate the child to using headphones gradually and then use only sparingly.

Weighty issues. Weighted clothing and other items can be a lifesaver for children with proprioceptive difficulties. They can help keep a hyperactive child calmer and in better control of his or her senses, resulting in increased attention, focus and learning. Therapy catalogs offer many options, but the cost can be prohibitive. Here are some creative, budget-friendly adaptations. Note: Use a weighted item only under the supervision of an occupational therapist, who can determine the appropriate weight. Too much weight can result in over-stimulation and/or injury.

- **Weighted vest for small budgets.** Catalog versions of the weighted vest can cost upwards of $65. Shop thrift stores or used sporting goods stores for a small fishing vest. If you are handy with a needle, you can make or modify an existing fashion vest by adding pockets either inside or outside for the weights. Weight the pockets with zip baggies of sand, rice, birdseed, etc. For stationary weight, use clay. (Be sure to remove weights before washing.)

- **Weighted blanket or quilt.** Denim is a naturally heavy fabric, so gather up the family's old, old jeans. Carefully remove the back pockets, then cut the leg fabric into 6" or 8" squares. Stitch together, then sew the pockets onto the quilt top in various places. Add batting and backing. The quilt will be heavy to begin with, but adding weight to the pockets can be a fun and beneficial activity for the child. What will go in the pockets? Pennies, pebbles, marbles? *Tip*: Consider how the child will use the quilt. If for sleeping, you'll want a larger size. A smaller size is good for TV-watching, reading and homework.

- **Hug chair.** Make two weighted "arms" (from pants leg or other fabric tube), then attach these to the arms of a chair.

Weighted "arms" wrap around or drape across child as she sits in the chair.

Bean bags. Bean bags are great sensory integration toys. Make a "family" from tube socks filled with different materials: beans, bubble wrap, nut shells—anything that has a different texture or makes a sound. Seal the end of the sock by tying a knot or stitching across. Make faces on the socks with paint or marker pen if that tickles your child.

- Bigger bean bags—use the sleeve of an old sweater or sweatshirt; stitch the ends shut.
- Even bigger bean bags—use a pant leg from sweatpants; stitch ends shut.

Fidget toys basket. The Oriental Trading Company (www.orientaltrading.com) catalog is a great source of inexpensive fidget toys. The only caveat is that they are usually sold in lots of a dozen, so you'll want to band together with several other parents and/or teachers to make your purchase. A fidget basket should contain items that stimulate many different senses: visual, auditory, olfactory, tactile, vestibular (rhythmic items), oral-motor (blowing toys). Some suggestions: Porcupine or koosh balls (especially those that glow in the dark), stretchy animals, glow tubes, mini-maracas, finger puppets, squeeze toys with bulgy eyes, jointed wiggle snakes, intertwined light balls, squishy yo-yos, handheld sport ball water game, finger poppers, mini kaleidoscopes, colored sand timers, tops, sticky "buddies," whistles, hand clappers and kazoos (check out their "noisemaker assortment," fifty pieces for $6.95 —2004 price), to name just a few.

Clothes horse. While many children delight in new clothes, your tactile-defensive child with autism may find them torturous. Hand-me-downs or clothes purchased at consignment shops, thrift shops or garage sales have the advantage of already having been laundered several times. They are "broken in"—they are softer, the sometimes smelly and scratchy factory-applied chemical sizing is gone, if the item was going to shrink it already has so you know its true size and it won't end up pinching or binding after one washing. Remove all tags that may scratch, and be glad that some manufacturers are moving to thermal-applied labels—no tags.

> *Tip:* hand-me-downs (or call them something else if you prefer: hand-overs, hand-offs or hand-acrosses—or don't call them anything other than "the sweater that came from Jenny") from a favorite sibling or cousin may carry special association for the child with ASD, whose social connections are sometimes limited.

Ask for your child's opinion. We know a mom who was simply mortified to find out that her son with ASD hated the jeans she was buying him to wear to school. They were extremely uncomfortable to him, stiff and heavy, but she had just assumed he would want to wear what the other kids wear. When she asked why he never told her he didn't like them, his answer was: "You never asked." Through an occupational therapist, she discovered that he really wanted to wear soft sweatpants and T-shirts—which was just fine with her. His teachers reported a noticeable decrease in his general agitation level following the shift to softer clothes.

Tactile invaders may include buttons, snaps, zippers, collars, cuffs, French seams, appliqués, tags, beads, sequins, ribbon or embroidery. Make sure to ask. It can ward off sensory problems and empower children by giving them choices.

More on clothes. If overstimulated visual perception is a problem, your child may prefer clothes in plain solid colors, clothes that are free of stripes, patterns, plaids, logos or prints. If you think he is not able to tell you, offer clothing choices and see what he chooses. Then honor it.

Children with a need for proprioceptive input (deep pressure) may be calmed by wearing snug leggings or tights, ace bandages or a close fitting vest.

Be aware of fabrics. If your child is chemical-sensitive, he may be more comfortable in natural fibers like cotton. Wool and linen are natural but can be scratchy. Polyester (including fleeces), rayon and nylon are synthetics and may retain heat more than cotton.

Your child and the blustery day. Windy weather can be, literally, hair-raising for your child, causing unpleasant sensations that can make him anxious or angry. Make sure he leaves the house with a suitable hat or cap on those breezy days, whether balmy or brr-r-r-r.

Dealing with "stims." Stims—self-stimulating behaviors such as hand-flapping, rocking or fidgeting—are a result of the child's disordered vestibular sense seeking motion. Trying to eliminate the stim is missing the point: There's a function to the stim that needs to be recognized and replaced with a socially appropriate behavior. Incorporating movement-seeking activities into their day at every opportunity can help significantly.

At school, let the student do these things: take the attendance or lunch count to the office, bring out the PE equipment, clean the chalkboard or erase board, stack chairs, carry books, pull on a piece of rubber tubing attached to his chair or backpack, rub a worry stone, climb or swing on playground equipment, hit a tether ball, play drums in music class or during classroom songs.

What's that funky smell? Children with autism may experience olfactory defensiveness, which means that their sense of smell is hyper-acute. Aromas, odors and smells that the typical population may enjoy or not even notice have the potential to make the child with autism miserable. Imagine a smell that makes you instantly nauseous, or that certain perfume that can give you a headache in five seconds flat; now imagine that happening all day long, every day, and you might begin to appreciate how extensively the olfactory sense can affect a child with ASD. If your child is olfactory defensive, here are some ways to make your home a friendlier place:

- Use perfume-free, dye-free laundry detergents and fabric softeners to launder his clothes, sheets and towels. Avoid bleach.

- Provide unscented, hypo-allergenic soaps for his bathtub or shower.

- Use an exhaust fan or light a candle to burn off unpleasant bathroom smells (yes, it works). Scented sprays only add another layer of odor.

- Use unscented hand lotions and deodorants. Avoid heavy perfumes, aftershaves, body gels, etc.

- Make sure the house is well ventilated when using ammonia, bleach and other heavily scented (such as lemon or pine) cleaning products.

- Ditto for cooking strong-smelling foods like fish or bacon. Use an exhaust fan, open the windows or choose a different food. Substitute raw vegetables for cooked if the odors offend.

- Store yard chemicals such as insecticides and fertilizers in a well-ventilated area away from your child's living space (i.e., so she doesn't have to walk by it every time she goes to the car).

- Experiment with aromatherapy to determine which scents calm her and which are agitating. Lavender, cinnamon, chamomile, vanilla and patchouli are common calming scents but your child may favor something completely different.

Did you know . . .

That our sense of smell can detect up to 400,000 odors? But noses get tired easily; that is why you can only smell a few roses at a time, or why that pool chlorine may be overwhelming when you walk in the door but fades after a few minutes—babies do not discriminate between "good" and "bad" smells until they observe our responses: bakery, yum! trash can, pew!—women have more perceptive olfactory systems than men.

Sleep on it. Sleep problems fill entire volumes even for neuro-typical kids, but be aware that sensory issues can affect this area of a child's life too. Children with autism may have atypical proprio-ceptive and/or vestibular issues contributing to their sleep difficul-ties. Here are some tactics that take those characteristics into account.

- Pajamas: Long-john type pajamas provide gentle pressure all over that may be comforting. Loose pajamas, nightgowns that ride up, fabrics that scratch or pill, buttons, ribbons or embroidery that scratches or produces bumps, and elastic around ankles or neck are all possible irritants.

- His sleeping space: Is his sleeping space so big he might not feel boundaries? Try a tent, canopy, or hanging curtain around the bed (ala Harry Potter, or a hospital room).

- A mummy-style sleeping bag or weighted blanket (consult an occupational therapist before using this) might help.

- Taking a "lovey" to bed is a common childhood practice, but the usual teddy bear or dolly may not be your child's lovey of choice. However odd, accommodate his preference, as long as it's safe. We know one child who adored his whisk broom and took it to bed with him every night.

- Rubbing your child with lotion before bed can provide great proprioceptive input, but beware of perfumes and scents that may bother him as he tries to go to sleep. Be especially aware of competing scents, e.g., soap, shampoo, lotion and toothpaste, all from the bedtime routine, may each have different perfumes that combine for a nauseating effect.

The human hamburger. Your little burger fanatic will love this sensory game that offers silliness in the form of proprioceptive, deep-pressure input. You'll need two floor or sofa pillows (the bun) and a large, soft paintbrush or car wash sponge (to add the condi-ments). Have your child (the burger) center himself on the bottom half of the bun (one of the pillows), then ask him what he likes on his burger—ketchup, mustard, relish? Spread on the condiments using the paintbrush or sponge, using firm pressure down his arms, legs and torso—no tickling! Then add another pillow as the top of the bun. (Do not cover the face or head.) Lean some of your weight on the "sandwich" and make chomping noises. Apply pressure to different parts of his body through the pillow. When you are done "eating" the burger—and you have told him how delicious it was—ask if he would like to be dessert now. An Oreo, or perhaps an ice cream sandwich?

Tea party to the max. Simple aromatherapy for the bath—if your child likes the scent of peppermint, chamomile or other herbal tea concoctions, give her a few tea bags to steep in the tub with her.

More bath fun. An old rotary egg beater and some liquid bubble bath, baby bath or dish soap combine for a fun sensory exercise. Whip up a bowl of bubbles, a towering tub of suds, a wading pool full of froth and a ferocious shark (or mermaid). Sensory integration and fine motor work—a perfect match.

Hair bbb-rr-uu-sss-hhh? Many children with autism enjoy vibrating toys, vibrating pens and even vibrating toothbrushes; the extra sensation sends important sensory input to the child's brain. Here's a less well-known item for the reluctant groomer: the vibrating hairbrush. Designed for "regular folks" as a scalp massager, OTs report using it successfully with children who simply hate having their hair brushed. Ask at a local beauty supply shop, or check online. Two sources: www.unwind.com and www.ballbeauty.com.

The not-so itsy-bitsy spider. What kid didn't love the scene in *The Parent Trap* where the twins ensnare their unwanted soon-to-be-stepmother in a web of string? Your little Spiderman will enjoy turning his room or playroom into a life-size web with a ball of string, yarn, kite string or even unwaxed dental floss. Wrap the string around doorknobs, dresser knobs, bed legs, chair spindles, anything sturdy. Have him crawl, climb through and otherwise navigate the maze. At the end of the day, give him scissors to cut his way out. Great sensory fun.

Punch it. A single-hole punch with or without padded grips is a good fine motor development tool for increasingly competent hands.

- Just learning: Punch colored sheets of paper randomly to make confetti for your next party.

- I'm mad: Have him work his angries out by giving him a picture of something he doesn't like (unfavorite food, bad guy from a movie, or just draw a mad face on a piece of paper) and telling him to punch it away.

- More advanced: Have him punch around the outline of a large drawing.

Summer fun, winter fun. Many of your favorite summer activities can be reinterpreted for winter. A few to get you started are listed below.

- Get out the beach toys you used to make sand castles and make snow castles instead; packed snow behaves much the same as packed wet sand.

- Rectangular food storage containers can be used to make bricks for forts and igloos.

- Write messages or draw pictures in the snow with a stick. Take a photo of your message ("I love Grandma") and put it in a photo snow globe as a special gift to a loved one. (Photo snow globes available at craft stores like Michael's.)

- Is your child a *Cat in the Hat* fan? Mix a few drops of red food coloring in a spray bottle and spray the snow pink, just like Little Cats A, B, C, D and E.

- A tire swing left over from summer makes for good snowball-throwing target practice.

- Or use that tire swing to let go and land in a mound of snow, instead of a pile of leaves.

- Practice that tennis or baseball swing with snowballs. If it splats, you know you hit it.

- Get out that slippery-slide and ice it down; use it as a bowling lane or shuffleboard alley.

    Remember: Children with autism are frequently insensitive to cold. Since they won't tell you when they get too cold, keep checking to make sure they are properly protected at all times.

Outdoor bracelet. Sturdy, sticky duct tape is the beginning of a neat outdoor bracelet. Tape it sticky-side-out around her wrist and let her fill it with sticks and leaves, sand and shell bits, grass and flower petals. Note: Will she melt down when you try to cut it off her later? Make the loop big enough that she can slip it off her hand.

Bring in the great outdoors. Some kids with ASD just don't enjoy the great outdoors because there are so many things "dirty" or yucky with which they come in contact. Acclimate them slowly and at their own pace by bringing the outdoors in. A small wading pool on your kitchen, bathroom or mud-room floor can become a mini-ecosystem. Dirt, sand, twigs, rocks, pinecones, nuts, seed pods, a square of sod can all be shoveled, sorted, stacked and otherwise manipulated from a safe spot in her inside world. She can wear plastic gloves to touch things at first. As they become more familiar to her, she may find it easier to transition to enjoying them outdoors.

Twelve warning signs of sensory overload. Ideas in this book and others, as well as suggestions from your OT and other professionals, provide you with myriad ways to enhance your child's over- or under-stimulated sensory systems. Some will be enjoyed and embraced by your child, others not.

It is natural to want your child to engage in enjoyable sensory activities "to the max," but do keep in mind: *Is more really better?* Emphatically no, say occupational therapists. Delicate senses can become overstimulated by too much of a good thing, triggering that dreaded meltdown. Would you know the warning signs of impending overstimulation? Familiarize yourself with these red flags:

1. Loss of balance or orientation

2. Skin flushes, or suddenly goes pale

3. Child is verbalizing "Stop!"

4. Child steadfastly refuses activity

5. Racing heartbeat, or, sudden drop in pulse

6. Hysteria, crying

7. Stomach distress: cramps, nausea, vomiting

8. Profuse sweating

9. Child becomes agitated or angry

10. Child begins repeating echolalic phrases, or some familiar non-relevant phrase over and over again (self-calming behavior)

11. Child begins stimming (repetitive, self-calming behaviors)

12. Child lashes out, hits or bites

If any of these occur, stop the activity at once and consult your occupational therapist as to how often and how much of the activity s/he recommends for your child.

To activity and beyond! Fifty ways to get them moving. Physical activity is critical to any child's overall health, and the social interaction provided by such pastimes can be very beneficial too. All physical activities will provide your child vestibular (movement and balance) and proprioceptive input (information from their joints regarding their body position.) Both of these types of sensory input are extremely powerful and organizing for the body. Even with the more impaired, over time their gross motor skills will get better. Feedback from other people (you, instructor or playmate) and from their own bodies will help them improve. When they do, you'll also see self-esteem skyrocketing.

In exploring physical activities for your child, liberate yourself from any constraints imposed by yourself or others as to what constitutes a legitimate "sport." Although many children with autism enjoy soccer, basketball and baseball, team sports are not for everyone. Myriad rules can be confusing, the jumble of bodies upsetting, the expectations of team members stressful.

Some parents (not you, of course) are of the mindset, often to the detriment of their child, that Bobby isn't playing a "real" sport unless he's on the school football team. As a concept, it simply isn't true. Our kids can excel at various activities when given the chance, gradual exposure and proper guidance. And there is a lot to be said for seeking out the less populated sports: They may be much more welcoming of beginners, even offering sample courses or mini-lessons. (*Tip*: If they don't, explain your situation and ask for one. The worst that can happen is they say no, and the manner in which they say no will give you an idea of whether or not your child will be welcomed there.) Many children thrive in the "big fish in a small pond" atmosphere of the lesser-known sport.

So if the concept of competition is too challenging for your child, let it go for now. There is every possibility he may grow into it later, and if not, building an association of physical activity with fun has a much more profound life impact.

Where you live will partially dictate your choice of activity. Denver denizens may find surfing difficult to pursue; ditto for aspiring skiers in Miami. But it's never an excuse for the truly motivated. Remember the 1988 Olympics and the Jamaican bobsled team? They were the masters of adapted sports, outfitting their bobsled with wheels to practice in their tropical locale. What everybody remembers about them is their spunk and their sense of fun, not that they finished last. Six years later in Lillehammer, they in fact finished ahead of both USA teams in the four-man event.

The list below suggests many and varied ways to enjoy sports and physical activity outside the typical arena of team sports. There is no magic about the list; it's comprised of regular activities that have been around forever.

What we want to impress upon you is that possibilities—lots of them—do exist and to not overlook the obvious when you're planning for physical recreation. They *can* do it. Pursued at an individual pace, these activities may give your child more room for growth and achievement, bettering your chances for both success and enthusiasm. In the marathon of life, isn't that real success, after all?

Water sports

- Swimming: swim lessons, swim team, synchronized swimming, aquacise for kids
- Diving
- Surfing/boogie boarding
- Rowing, canoeing, rafting

Fun on wheels

- Big Wheel
- Tricycle
- Bicycle with training wheels
- Two-wheeler
- Alley cat
- Tandem
- Scooter
- Roller skates—four-wheel or inline
- Skateboard

Racket sports

- Tennis
- Racquetball
- Handball
- Badminton
- Ping-Pong (table tennis)

"Take-aim" sports

- Bowling
- Golf

- Miniature golf (putt-putt)
- Archery

Running/walking/jumping

- Kids' biathalon or triathalon
- Jogging
- Trampoline
- Hiking

Snow sports

- Downhill skiing
- Cross-country (Nordic) skiing
- Snowboarding
- Tobogganing
- Snow-shoeing
- Ice skating —figure or speed

Martial arts

- Tai chi, tae kwon do, karate, judo, aikido, kick-boxing, capoeira

Equestrian

- Horseback riding
- Kids rodeo

Play activities

- Jumping rope
- Hop/jump balls (handle on top)
- Hula hoops
- Tether ball
- Pogo stick
- Jai-alai (scoop-toss games) or Velcro®-disk catch games
- Lawn or floor hockey
- Frisbee

Class instruction
- Tap dancing
- Ballet
- Hip-hop or ethnic dance
- Jazz or modern dance
- Yoga
- Baton twirling
- Gymnastic/tumbling

Chapter 2

The Limits of My World

Communication and Language Strategies and Considerations

The limits of my language mean the limits of my world.

Ludwig Wittgenstein

The eyes have it? Consider for a moment how easily typical kids capture our attention with eye contact and pointing. It's therefore understandable that we view these as the most obvious demonstrations of interest towards an object or a person. Most kids with autism, however, have difficulty indicating interest. Their challenged sensory systems can interfere with visual processing and their motor systems can't plan, coordinate and execute in a way that produces the spontaneous gaze or gesture.

The pearl of wisdom here is this: We can't rely on what kids with autism do or don't do *from a movement perspective* as an accurate gauge of their interests, inner thoughts and feelings.

In the absence of a point or eye gaze, we need to look for other clues that signal interest. It might be a glance in the direction of an object, a squeal of delight or a particular part of a video the child plays over and over. It could be as simple (and silent) as a turn of the head every time something of interest is mentioned. When we become careful observers and listeners, we will see their attempts to convey interest and uncover the clues that tell us what to acknowledge, respond to and teach.

Just ask. The author's barely-verbal four-year-old came home from his preschool (a supported integrated social communication classroom) one day and said:

> *"You wan' know someting?"*

> *"Yes, of course," I responded, delighted that it appeared he was going to spontaneously offer something he had learned at school.*

> *"You wan' know someting, Mom?"*

> *"Yes! Yes, I want to know something," I enthused.*

"You wan' know someting?" This went on for several exchanges with me starting to wilt around the edges because I clearly wasn't giving the "right" response. Finally he said, and with a great deal of pride:

"Well, you wan' know someting, just axsk me!"

We forget to "just ask" the child with limited language, perhaps under a partially misguided assumption that he can't tell us, or worse, doesn't have an opinion or preference.

Just ask—the student with autism learns in ways that may not be typical or common. Teachers, let him help you teach. Ask him how he feels he learns best, and listen to the response (which may not be verbal). Is it through reading or writing? By working with a peer? Through field trips, or through hands-on activities like science experiments, art projects or board games?

By asking the child to think about how he learns and what helps him learn, he takes a step toward accepting some responsibility for his own learning. Such awareness can be empowering.

Do you hear what I hear? When language impairments exist, a child's hearing should be tested to rule out physiological problems. The child with autism may have difficulty with the typical school-administered test, wherein the student dons headphones and is asked to raise his hand in response to differently pitched tones. He may not understand the instructions and simply take visual cues from the other children around him, raising his hand when they do, or doing so randomly in an attempt to give the expected response.

You may wish to consult a pediatric audiologist, a specialist in assessing hearing loss in children. Audiologists may be M.A.s or Ph.D.s, and go through a similar credential process as speech pathologists. Look for certifications from the American Speech Language Hearing Association (CCC-A) or Fellows of the American Academy of Audiology (F-AAA).

There are several different kinds of testing, based on the child's developmental and chronological age. The audiologist can work with your doctor, teacher and speech/language pathologists to determine appropriate choices. Behavioral response tests like the one described above can be modified for children as young as infants. Auditory brainstem response (ABR) testing or otoacoustic emissions (OAE) testing measures nerve response in the ear. Tympanometry measures eardrum movement and is useful in detecting problems such as fluid behind the ear.

It's more than a keyboard. Assistive technology (AT) is a related service available within IDEA that helps students with ASD achieve goals and outcomes that might have previously not been attainable because of their limited language/communication abilities. The use of an AT item, such as a communication board, a computer, or a DynaVox is not the goal in itself—a relevant and meaningful support strategy that covers all facets of the child's life is what it's all about.

What type of strategy and technology might be helpful to a particular student? According to www.closingthegap.com, a useful website on various AT issues, professionals evaluating a child and a particular activity for AT might ask themselves the following questions:

- What are classmates expected to do in this activity?
- What is the student with autism expected to do?
- What are the learning goals for this activity?
- How can this particular student best access the information, i.e., what's his learning style?
- How can we check that learning has actually taken place?
- What are the student's strengths and how can we use these strengths in this activity?

If you think AT would benefit your child with ASD, ask your child's school administration for an Assistive Technology evaluation to determine the supports and systems that could best help your child succeed within the educational environment.

Attention, please. As adults, we often forget to establish contact with a child before we begin speaking or initiate conversation. Words fly out of our mouths and we expect our kids or students to understand that we're talking to them. Children with autism generally lack social referencing skills, making it imperative that we get their attention before initiating conversation. Try these simple ideas:

- Physically move to the student's level. Walk over to the child, sit, bend or squat to get your face at the child's eye level.
- Establish attention. Get physically close, if tolerated. Put yourself in the child's line of vision, even if it means moving his or your seat. Watch for the student to orient to you and realize that doesn't necessarily mean eye contact. Become animated—even to the point of becoming silly; use visual props.
- Let the child know that what follows merits her attention. This could be a simple verbal or visual cue: a tap on her shoulder or arm, saying the child's name or a preparatory word or phrase, such as "listen", "watch" or "look at me."
- Use gestures and body language meaningfully. Avoid waving your hands around in the air while you talk; use gestures and body movements in a slow, pronounced way so the child has time to really make the association.

Jump right in. Often children with autism can be so engrossed in their thoughts that they start conversation mid-stream, making it difficult for a listener to follow: ". . . and there was a girl in a green dress, so pretty, and then a frog came in!" Because they lack Theory of Mind skills, these children assume the listener already knows what he is thinking about and can fill in the blanks.

What to do: Probe—at length and with patience. Ask him, "What are you talking about? What happened? Is it a book, is it a movie, is it real? Did it happen yesterday or today?" Have the child go back to the beginning of the thought, but keep in mind that this may be very frustrating for him. He may not want to take the time to go back to the beginning or he may not be sure where the beginning was.

The bottom line is that he does not know what the listener does or doesn't know. Resist the temptation to say or think, "Okay, whatever" and move on. Don't let him "get away" with substituting random thoughts for comprehensible conversation.

Feed language in. Here's a scenario that may be familiar to many parents and teachers. A child can articulate the first and last word of a sentence, but everything in between is unintelligible, such as "The cat ah-do-nee-durn-nee-bont the fence" for "The cat ran and jumped over the fence." Or, even more simply, "I ah-ah go ah-ah-ah store," for "I want to go to the store." In both cases, the child knows that more words are needed but can't come up with them, so she inserts a "marker."

What do to: Feed the language in: "Oh, you want to go to the store!"

Vocabulary game. Play this in a semi-darkened room. Give the child or children a flashlight and have them find and illuminate objects or words as you call them out.

Moving beyond single words. Shelley speaks in one-word sentences such as "Cup." To help Shelley move beyond these single word utterances, model the full sentence, "I want the cup," and have the child echo it back to you.

> *Activity*: Choose a photo to talk about. It can be one of yours, or one from a book or magazine. Have the child describe something in the picture. Take turns adding more and more detail. The conversation might build something like this:

Boy.

Boy with a ball.

The boy's ball is black and white.

The boy is playing soccer with the black and white ball.

The boy is going to kick the soccer ball.

The boy kicking the ball is wearing a green shirt.

The green shirt is because his team is called the Dragons.

He is number 3 on the Dragons.

The Dragons are playing outside.

It is a sunny day.

His face is happy.

You may want to start a card file of pictures and photos from which to choose to do this activity. Return to each photo more than once to build on previous conversations. And be patient. The process of going from the original one-word description to a full paragraph may be months or even years.

Visual strategies. Most children with ASD are visual learners, that is, they more easily understand what they see than what they hear. However, the majority of our educational and social interactions take place through verbal communication, resulting in numerous opportunities daily for communication breakdowns to occur.

Supplementing verbal communication with visual tools can help. What are visual tools? According to Linda Hodgdon, visual strategy guru within the autism field, they are anything the student can see. Visual schedules, choice boards, communication strips, classroom rules, step-by-step written directions, even body movements can all make a significant difference in a student's ability to participate successfully at school or at home. Visual tools assist students in processing language, organizing their thinking and remembering information. They can help students learn appropriate social interaction and positive behaviors.

Visual schedules and calendars are the most common visual tools used for children with ASD. They range from simple to complex and can be used within all environments (e.g., classroom/gym/music room, in OT or speech therapy, at home or church, etc.). The benefits of using visual schedules are many:

- Visual schedules clarify that activities happen within a specific time period and help children understand the concept of sequencing.

- They alert the student to any changes in the daily routine.

- Visual schedules are effective in helping a student transition independently between activities and environments by showing where he is to go next.

- They lessen the anxiety level of children with autism, and thus reduce the possible occurrence of challenging behaviors, by providing the structure for the student to organize and predict daily and weekly events.

- Visual supports can also increase a student's motivation to complete less desired activities by strategically alternating more preferred with less-preferred activities on the student's individual visual schedule.

- Social interactions can be incorporated into a daily schedule: showing completed work to a teacher, saying hello and goodbye, asking a peer to play, etc.

- For non-verbal students a visual schedule can be a way to introduce symbols that the student can eventually use as an alternate form of communication. Through the consistent use of the schedule, the student can begin to pair the symbols presented with the activities that are occurring.

How to create a visual schedule

1. Decide who will use the schedule: several people (i.e., a general schedule) or a single child?

2. Divide the day or the activity into segments and name each segment.

3. Choose the visual system you will use, based on the child's level of representation.

4. Think about how and when the schedule will be used, and select an appropriate format. A schedule for many students will probably be larger and posted on a wall. An individual schedule for a single child might be desk sized or even smaller, to fit into his notebook and carry with him.

5. Select appropriate visuals that pertain to the activity or the day and create the schedule.

   Tip: A minimum of two scheduled items should be presented at a time so that the student begins to understand that events and activities happen in a sequential manner, not in isolation.

6. Walk through the schedule before introducing it to the child to make sure it is clear, sequential and that no parts are missing.

7. Teach the student how to use the schedule. Make sure she understands each visual representation used.

8. Refer to the schedule often to provide information about what is happening, what is changing, and anything else he needs to know.

Before using that visual schedule. Using visual schedules with a child with autism is a positive teaching practice. It capitalizes on their visual thinking and can alleviate stress in even a more advanced-functioning child. (Think of the comfort level your Daytimer or activity calendar provides you.) However, an effective and functional visual schedule is more than just placing pictures in a sequence.

Have your speech pathologist or autism specialist determine your child's level of representation. What is meaningful—photos, drawings, words? Then, have an occupational therapist assist in determining how your child best tracks the visual. Is it top to bottom, or left to right? How many items should appear on the schedule? Three may be the maximum for some children; others may be able to handle six or more.

Visual crutches? Your student with autism is using a visual schedule to manage his day at school and you've seen his self-esteem and independence skyrocket. Things are going so well, in fact, that you think the schedule is no longer needed. Rethink this idea. Visual schedules are not temporary aides to be faded out. They should be viewed, instead, as management tools that help students stay organized, calm and functioning efficiently. As the child's representation skills change, so should the format of the schedule, from photos to drawings to words. However, for the student with autism, the consistent use of a visual schedule is an extremely important skill. It has the potential to increase independent functioning throughout his life—at school, home and in the community.

Expressive or receptive? The primary function of a visual schedule is to give information to a student, depicted through photos, illustrations or text, about a series of events. It is a receptive communication tool in that it helps the student comprehend messages provided by others. Verbal conversation may take place; however, it is ancillary to the primary purpose of the schedule.

Choice boards, by their definition, require an expressive response. A choice board or choice display is a visual two- or three-dimensional representation of the choice possibilities. Photos, text or tangible objects can be used. Choice boards are effective in giving the child with autism an extended opportunity to reply. Under normal circumstances, a verbal choice, "Do you want juice or milk?" is over in a couple of seconds. Supplementing the verbal message with a graphic representation gives the student with autism additional time to process the message and be successful in responding.

Give your child extra time to talk. Children with ASD often have a delayed response time. Listening, comprehending and then speaking does not always happen within nanoseconds, as it does for NT kids. They need extra time to formulate what they want to say. Don't rush in to repeat the question or comment, or finish their sentences for them. Wait a few extra seconds for them to respond.

If you're relatively certain they know the word but can't come up with it, you can feed in the language by offering a choice: "Were you saying that you wanted the turkey sandwich or the peanut butter sandwich?"

Say what you mean, mean what you say. An effective communicator with kids with ASD will keep in mind that they think in literal and concrete ways, and that they tend to think specific to general, rather than general to specific. Help them better understand the world around them by becoming cognizant of the ambiguities that regularly fill our conversations. Sloppy talk is confusing for a child who is analyzing your every word to get the full meaning of your conversation. Speak plainly, speak in complete thoughts, and speak in the positive.

SAY	RATHER THAN
This is a picture of a dog.	This is a dog.
Put the flowers in the vase.	Put these in there.
It's a red sweater.	It's red.
After you finish your math you can go to recess.	If you don't finish your math, you can't go to recess.
Please walk to the classroom.	No running in the halls.
Put your hands in your pockets.	Keep your hands to yourself (a figure of speech. He's thinking: where else would they be?)
We are going home now.	Let's get going.

Trampoline fun. Speech therapists, OTs and many parents recognize the benefits a trampoline can provide in helping children with ASD regulate their sensory input, decompress when needed and even encourage voice development and language. Even with verbal kids, there's more to do on that bounding mat than just jumping. Draw letters and/or shapes on a trampoline with regular sidewalk chalk. Have the child jump from one letter or shape to another. Go on to create fun and educational variations:

- Jump from letter to letter to spell out a word
- Jump from one shape to another in a preplanned order, or spontaneously as the therapist or child shouts it out
- Print words on the trampoline. Jump from word to word to create a phrase or a sentence.

Wordless books. Wordless books are a valuable resource for children facing language impairments. They may be narrative, non-fiction or conceptual in nature. In addition to introducing or stimulating book enjoyment in general, wordless books are remarkable tools for building both oral and written language, developing vocabulary and critical thinking. "Reading" the book allows children to create stories as they go along. It can be very empowering for the child to "control" the story; because there are no words, his interpretation is the "right" one—a boon for developing self-esteem alongside other skills. And there can be more than one "right" way to tell the story, if she chooses.

Four tips to get you started:
- Many genres of wordless books are included in the list that follows. Some children with autism are very concrete thinkers and are not comfortable with fantasy scenarios or anthropomorphic animals that talk or act in "human" ways. Nonfiction wordless books or narratives about real-life children and animals may be best for them. Other kids may reject realism and go only for fantasy, which is why the next tip is so important.

- Preview a book before you share it with your child. You want to be sure ahead of time that the content is appropriate for his age level, life experience, attention span and interests.

- For younger children, familiar themes are best, such as cars or pets. As they grow older, less familiar themes such as space travel and foreign cultures can be introduced more successfully.

- Use the age recommendations on these books only as the loosest of guides. They are a gauge for typically-developing children and may or may not have any relevance to your child.

Suggested reading:

The Patchwork Farmer by Craig McFarland Brown
All ages

The Mystery of the Giant Footprints by Fernando Krahn
Ages baby-preschool

Beach Day by Helen Oxenbury
Ages 18 mos.-3 years

Tabby: A Story in Pictures by Aliki
Ages 2-5

Do You Want To Be My Friend? by Eric Carle
Ages 2-5

I Can't Sleep by Philippe Dupasquier
Ages 2-5

Moonlight by Jan Ormerod
Ages 2-5

Mouse Numbers by Jim Arnosky
Ages 3-6

Amanda's Butterfly by Nick Butterworth
Ages 3 and up

Truck by Donald Crews
Ages 3-6

Pancakes for Breakfast by Tomie DePaola
Ages 3-6

A Boy, a Dog and a Frog by Mercer Mayer
Ages 3-6

Picnic by Emily Arnold McCully
Ages 3-6

Look! Look! Look! by Tana Hoban
Ages 3-7

10 Minutes till Bedtime by Peggy Rathman
Ages 3-6

Dinosaur! by Peter Sis
Ages 3-6

You Can't Take a Balloon Into the Metropolitan Museum
by Jacqueline Preiss Weitzman   Ages 3-8

The Bear and the Fly by Paula Winter
Ages 3-6

The Bear by Raymond Briggs
Ages 4-8

Building by Elisha Cooper
Ages 4-8

Good Dog, Carl by Alexandra Day
Ages 4-8

Shrewbettina's Birthday by John Goodall
Ages 4-8

Good Night, Garden Gnome by Jamichael Henterly
Ages 4-8

Changes, Changes by Pat Hutchins
Ages 4-8

Rain by Peter Spier
Ages 4-8

Look-Alikes by Joan Steiner
Ages 4-8

Anno's Journey by Mitsumasa Anno
Ages 5-9

Free Fall by David Wiesner
Ages 5-9

A Day, a Dog by Gabrielle Vincent
Ages 8-14

Enjoying wordless books with your child: Eight ideas

1. First, look at the cover of the book and try to make a prediction as to what the book will be about. Look at each page and ask the child questions about how the pictures in the book relate to him.

2. Ask lots of "wh" questions—who, what, when, where, why. Phrase the questions beginning with "I wonder": I wonder why he is scared? I wonder what is going to happen after she opens the door? I wonder what he is saying to her?

3. Have your child make up a story to go with the pictures (use answers to the "I wonder" questions as a basis), then write the story down to read back later. Older children can write the story themselves, with a greater eye for detail.

4. Have your child make up names for the characters.

5. If the book is a narrative story, introduce sequencing: What happened *first*? What happened *next*? What happened *last*? Talk about how the story has a beginning, a middle and an end.

6. Explore feelings and emotions. Have your child try to decide how the characters are feeling by looking at their faces and body language. Build a vocabulary of emotions: happy, sad, anxious, scared, proud, disgusted, angry, shy, disappointed, excited, confused, etc. Keep the list age-appropriate.

7. Most of these authors have released multiple books; if your child enjoys one, explore them all.

8. Check your library or bookstore for video versions of some of these books, and other wordless stories. Here are a few:

The Red Balloon

The Remarkable Runaway Tricycle

A Boy, A Dog and a Frog / Frog Goes to Dinner / Frog on His Own

Raymond Briggs' The Bear

Amelia Bedelia.

The Amelia Bedelia books by Peggy Parish enjoy a large following of readers who find them amusing. Is Amelia Bedelia an adult with autism? She is certainly the ultimate concrete thinker, interpreting to the letter instructions like "draw the curtains in the afternoon" and "giving Miss Alma a (baby) shower."

We've seen children with similar autism traits react very differently to Amelia Bedelia. Some identify strongly with her: "Why does she keep getting in trouble? She's right!" The author's son, a very concrete thinker, is nevertheless infuriated with her: "She's stupid!" Another child we know, coming from a similar place on the spectrum, finds the physical humor hilarious, such as Amelia's responding to an order to "change the towels in the bathroom" by cutting them up. He has to stop and think twice to pick up the double meaning of the phrase. There is no "correct" interpretation of Amelia Bedelia. If your child likes her, enjoy. If not, move on.

Environment can impact speech development. Much of our speech is learned imitatively, and a child who is not frequently exposed to other speaking people will develop speech more slowly. In addition, self-contained special education classrooms may not provide many opportunities for neuro-typical peer language modeling. Parents and language professionals should actively seek outlets for a child where he will be exposed to typically-developing kid talk.

Tips for encouraging speech and conversation. Maintaining a language-rich environment day to day is one of the best way parents and teachers can encourage speech and conversation. Here are a few simple ways to do that.

- Send your child's teacher or speech pathologist a note each Monday listing three things your child did over the weekend.

Ask that they engage the child in conversation about these things.

- Answer your child every time he speaks to you, letting him know you value everything he has to say. Look at him when you speak to him.

  Tip: Do this for the nonverbal child as well. A paraeducator's story: "I worked with a child who made non-word sounds over and over. Different shushing cues didn't work. So I tried repeating his sounds. He looked at me and stopped. I asked specialists if they thought this was "making fun" of his sounds, and they quickly assured me that it wasn't. He most likely thought I was listening to him and acknowledging that I had heard him. I hope so. It often helped."

- For the child who asks a continuous stream of questions, parroting the question back to him may break the cycle, especially if he already knows the answer. Child: "Are we going to PE?" Adult: "Aaron, are we going to PE?" Child: "Yes!"

- Or, break the stream of questions with a visual: Draw three simple squares/boxes on a piece of paper. Tell the child, "You get to ask me that question three times." When she asks, "Are we reading *Charlotte's Web* today?" respond with, "Yes. Now that's once you have asked," and show her you are crossing off one square. When you get to three, tell her, "Okay, that is three times and now we are not going to talk about it again." Then change the subject.

- Singing is speech. If your child learns songs easily, use that strength to enhance his language skills. Talk about any new words in the song he may not understand. Distinguish nonsense words from "real" words.

- Don't correct grammar or pronunciation. Just model the correct way. Child: "He didn't wented to the store." Adult: "No, he sure didn't go to the store."

Beware of idioms in your speech. An idiom is a phrase made up of words not used in their literal sense. "That's the way the cookie crumbles" is used to convey, "that's the way it happens." Daily English language is littered with thousands of idioms, many of which you may not even be aware you are using. To a child with ASD, with his concrete, literal way of thinking, these idioms are incomprehensible. The visual picture he creates upon hearing "It broke my heart" or "You're playing with fire" is probably quite disturbing.

American idioms:

American idioms fill entire books, but here are some more common ones, just to help you become aware of how prolific they are in conversation:

Animal idioms:

A little bird told me; you're in the doghouse; cat got your tongue?; the early bird catches the worm; buzz off; running around like a chicken with its head cut off; a bird in the hand is worth two in the bush; scaredy cat.

Body idioms:

It cost me an arm and a leg; it made my blood boil; I'm so hungry I could eat a horse; you're pulling my leg; break a leg; his eyes were popping out of his head; keep your eye out; shake a leg; I see the light; butt out.

Clothing idioms:

At the drop of a hat; he wore only his birthday suit; that was below the belt.

Color idioms:

He's feeling blue; they're green with envy; it looks black-and-white to me; she's tickled pink at his invitation; he's seeing red; Aunt Jane has a green thumb.

Heart idioms:

Big heart; by heart; lose my heart; from the bottom of my heart; with all my heart.

Initials:

ASAP; PDQ; IOU; FYI; TTFN.

Medical idioms:

Give him a dose of his own medicine; go under the knife; running a temperature; take a turn for the worse; be under the weather.

Money idioms:

Burn a hole in one's pocket; chicken feed; cheapskate; deadbeat; dime a dozen; feel like a million bucks; put in your two cents' worth.

Number idioms:

Looking after #1; two heads are better than one; six feet under; dressed to the nines.

Idioms are frequently the last language element new or struggling language learners understand, yet they are commonly used in conversation. This can create great confusion for the child with autism. Learning devices are available to help acclimate your child or student to idioms, but in the meantime, try to minimize them in your conversations. Convey your message using the plain, literal words.

Go Fish for idioms. Commercial versions of idiom games are available on the Internet, ranging in price from $5.95 upwards of $20. The Idiom Card Set, $5.95 from www.didax.com is an inexpensive one to try. A creative way to teach idioms (age 9 or so and up) is to make your own version of the "Go Fish" game.

Materials Needed: index cards, marker, list of idioms and meanings

1. Write idioms on one index card and the matching meaning on a second card

2. Make an answer key to be used during the game

3. Laminate the pieces for durability

4. Provide a manila envelope for storage

5. Write the instructions for the game on the outside of the envelope

Some suggested idioms to use in the Go Fish game: (Thousands more are available from Internet sources and books.)

- kick the bucket—die
- on cloud nine—extremely happy
- know the ropes—to understand what to do
- a wolf in sheep's clothing—a person who is really mean pretending to be nice
- stick out one's neck—try something risky
- through thick and thin—always a friend even if things get bad
- look a gift horse in the mouth—expressing ingratitude in response to someone's kind action
- out of the frying pan and into the fire—going from one bad event to something even worse
- a piece of cake—doing something that is very easy
- a chip off the old block —acting or looking like one's parent
- let the cat out of the bag—tell a secret
- eager beaver—a person who is very anxious or excited about doing something
- jump the gun—starting something before you are supposed to
- pull the wool over one's eyes—trick someone
- mind one's P's and Q's—being sure to behave properly
- one-horse town—very small town
- being chicken—afraid to do something

- a green thumb—able to make plants grow and look beautiful
- to split hairs—being extra "picky" about what is done or said
- go out on a limb—doing or saying something that could end in trouble

Game Instructions:
(can be played one-on-one or with multiple players)

1. Deal five cards to each player

2. The person to the right of the dealer goes first

3. Each player asks someone else for a card to match either the idiom or the meaning

4. A player must surrender the matching card if s/he has it

5. If there is no match, a card is drawn from the deck and play moves to the next person

6. Pairs of cards are laid on the table when there is a match

7. At the conclusion of the game, the answer key is used to check for correct matches

Phrasal verbs are like idioms in that they can evoke disturbing or confusing associations for the child with autism. Instead of, "I wish you hadn't brought that up," say, "I don't want to talk about that right now." Instead of "I said he could go but I had to take it back," say "I said he could go but then I had to tell him no." "Pass it off" means pretend or fake, "put it off" means stall or procrastinate. "Nod off" means fall asleep, "fall through" means not happen. Remember: Try to keep conversation simple and concrete.

Homophones. Homophones—two words that sound the same but have different meanings, like pale and pail—can be utterly confusing and therefore frustrating to your child. Patient repetition over time may be the only solution. You can offer a book like *The King Who Rained* by Fred Gwynne, wherein a little girl imagines such incongruous sights as "a king who rained for forty years", "the foot prince in the snow", "bear feet" and "fairy tails." If the child appears disconcerted by it, put it away for a while. Many typical children aren't ready for homophones until age nine or so.

Multiple learning channels. Turn on the closed-captioning while your child is watching a video. It reinforces spelling.

Photos before drawings. Many kids on the spectrum understand that a photograph is a visual representation of a person or object or scene, but don't make the connection to a two-dimensional line drawing. Consider which option is more appropriate for your child or student when using visual communication tools, such as picture cards or visual schedules. While a child is in his early learning stages, a digital camera can be a wise investment to snap those shots that will aid in language and communication development.

Repetitive-language stories. Children with autism value predictability and familiar routine. Books that incorporate repetitive language provide them with a sense of competency, whether they are actually reading, or just reciting the story from memory.

Stories that are especially good are those wherein the recurring words are language they can apply to real life. Example: "Not by the hair on my chinny chin chin!" is repeated throughout the *Three Little Pigs* story, but is not likely to come up in everyday conversation. By contrast, Pat Hutchins' *The Doorbell Rang* uses phraseology and a situation common enough for even small children to relate to in real life.

Here are some ideas for using repetitive language books.

- After the first couple of readings, tell your child you will be "taking turns" reading the story. You begin, and when you get to the repetitive phrase, stop and indicate that it is her turn to finish the sentence or "fill in the blank". Use a visual or tactile prompt if necessary, such as pointing to her or patting her hand.

- Your child may memorize entire books and "read" them back to you. Applaud this as you would "real" reading. It can be a key piece of the development of literacy skills.

- Choose books whose repeated language is relatively simple, at least at first. Cumulative repeated language stories such as *The Old Woman Who Swallowed a Fly* may be too fanciful, frightening or confusing.

Suggested reading:

Who Sank the Boat? by Pamela Allen

Do You Know What I'll Do? by Charlotte Zolotow

King Bidgood's in the Bathtub by Audrey and Don Wood

The Doorbell Rang by Pat Hutchins (and other titles by this author)

Something from Nothing by Phoebe Gilman

A Dark, Dark Tale by Ruth Brown

The Important Book by Margaret Wise Brown

It Looked Like Spilt Milk by Charles G. Shaw

Encouraging reading —what parents can do at home. Many, many teachers tell us that reading to your child at home is the single most important element in developing literacy. One teacher even told us that it is more important than anything they do at school. If you aren't currently reading to your child on a regular basis, start now.

- If reading every day seems overwhelming, start with two days a week and work up from there.

- It is not uncommon for children with autism to have as much as four grade levels discrepancy between their decoding skills and their comprehension skills. Decoding is not reading, although it is an essential element of reading. Decoding without comprehension is merely a recitation of syllables. When reading to your child at home, emphasize content and comprehension more than error-free recital of words. Correcting every little error discourages enjoyment in reading by turning it into work. So:

- Overlook errors. Teachers say, let us deal with that at school.

- If you must correct, do it in a way that doesn't sound like criticism: Just repeat the word the correct way in a positive tone of voice as if you didn't even notice it was wrong, and move along quickly.

- Probe for comprehension by asking questions. "How do you think the Little Engine feels? Have you ever felt like that?" But keep interruptions infrequent so the child doesn't lose the story line.

- If your child's teacher requires twenty or thirty minutes of home reading each night, remember that it doesn't have to be all at once. Two ten-minute sessions or several five-minute sessions may be infinitely more manageable. The cumulative effort is no less valuable than at a sustained sitting.

- Reading doesn't have to be in a chair or a bed. If you like reading in the bathtub, your child might, too.

Books as movies.

A lot of wonderful classic literature may be beyond the reading comprehension level of your child. But if a movie version exists, it can serve as a wonderful introduction to the story and may even motivate your child to want to read the book or have you read with him. Go beyond *Harry Potter* and discover *20,000 Leagues Under the Sea*, *Treasure Island*, *In Search of the Castaways*, *Heidi*, *Tom Sawyer*, *The Secret Garden*, *Anne of Green Gables*, *The Wizard of Oz*, *Moby Dick*, *The Jungle Book*, *Black Beauty*.

Profanity. Children with limited vocabularies and therefore limited means of verbally expressing themselves may be quite intrigued by the reaction they get when using cuss words or toilet talk. Here are some common sense ways to deal with the situation.

- Nip it in the bud by interceding at first incident. Calmly state, "We do not use that word in our family" and explore what might have provoked its use.

- If it came from anger or frustration, provide your child with a slate of suitable alternative expressions. Humor may work wonders in this area. Some families come up with their own personal expletives: "Oh, crudmuffins!" or "Oh, shittake mushrooms!" or "Oh, pluck a duck."

- Or substitute a comically pretentious word. The author's four-year-old son astonished more than a few adults in his day by bellowing *"Abomination!"* when frustrated.

- Set the tone by monitoring your own language. If adults and teens in the family tend toward colorful talk, many families have had success with a "Cussing Cup" or jar. Each offense requires a $.25 donation. When the jar is full the family decides upon a deserving charity. The "fine" is intended to create awareness, which then hopefully translates into behavior change.

- To use the cussing cup with a child, give him ten dimes (or twenty pennies or something else he likes) at the beginning of each week. Each potty word requires a donation to the cup. Whatever is left over at the end of the week is his to keep.

Almost as easy as 1-2-3. For the child with ASD, learning to write requires mastery of certain fine motor skills that you may have taken for granted. Executing a mature pencil grip and applying the proper amount of pressure from pencil to paper are tasks that do not come naturally or easily to many autism-challenged young people. Arduous though it may be for them, there is yet another element equally essential: motivation.

Pushing themselves to conquer the difficult task of writing may seem pointless if they cannot assign any relevance or significance to the abstract numerals, characters and shapes on a page that they are being asked to reproduce. This is not exactly a momentous thought; most of us would not be enthusiastic about performing a complex rote task if we did not see any end value in it. The need for relevance is pronounced in autism. So, first break down the mechanics of writing into understandable pieces. Then, give him a reason to write.

To help your child or student learn to write, use a three-step method:

- You write, for instance, his name (or other word or phrase interesting to him) lightly on lined paper and he traces over it.
- You write the name or phrase and he copies it on the line below or beside.
- He writes it independently.

To provide motivation and encouragement for writing, have him trace, copy or write you a note when he wants something special: "Can we go to the video store today?" or "I would like __ for my birthday" or "May I have chicken for dinner?"

Such notes will probably not cover the entire alphabet, but you may find him more willing to work on alphabet drills once he sees there is something in it for him.

Communication objectives for an IEP. Knowing what goals or objectives to include on an IEP is difficult, especially if your school is less than cooperative or not fully knowledgeable about the IEP process. Communication is a bedrock issue for almost all children with ASD. Myriad other difficulties can spring from the child's inability to communicate needs and wants—or, conversely, myriad other difficulties can be addressed by comprehensive language/communication therapy. Don't be placated by assertions that the child's language skills are fine simply because his enunciation is clear. Diction is only one component of the very, very complex science of language and communication. Even with the nonverbal child, there needs to exist a functional communication system in order for the child to benefit from other forms of instruction and decrease potential behavioral issues.

Here are twenty-five suggestions for short-term objectives in the area of speech communication, for the child who already is verbal. "Short- term" means the goal is achievable within the course of one school year. Remember that IEP goals must include measurable, quantifiable criteria as well as methods of evaluation and frequency. For example, using the first suggestion below:

Short-term objective: Child will answer when, how, why (because . . .) and whose (your, my, mine) questions.

Criteria: Four or five opportunities, with 90% accuracy

Evaluation method: Speech/language pathologist and teacher, by observation and probing for mastery of objectives

Schedule: Quarterly or end of each grading period or ongoing

1. Child will answer when, how, why (because . . .) and whose (your, my, mine) questions.

2. Child will answer comparative questions (which is heavier/lighter, slower/faster).

3. Child will describe a two-step or three-step procedure (First I . . ., then I . . . .).

4. Child will arrange three pictures in sequence to tell a story about a person, an action and an object.

5. Child will accurately use spatial terms: under, over, behind, in front.

6. Child will accurately use temporal terms: first, last, yesterday, tomorrow.

7. Child will stay on topic for (3, 4, 5) exchanges with a conversation partner.

8. Child will accurately use pronouns in conversation: I, they, he, she, his, her.

9. Child will describe attributes of objects: size (bigger, smaller, long, short, tiny, huge), texture (rough, smooth), color.

10. Child will describe functions of objects (I use this to . . .).

11. Child will describe parts of an item (It has a red handle and a round wheel.).

12. Child will comprehend four new vocabulary words for each new classroom theme (tides/crustacean/ocean/gills, veins/skeleton/organ/muscle).

13. Child will describe emotions (angry, frustrated, sad, excited).

14. Child will learn to protest appropriately ("Not now please.").

15. Child will verbally respond, in an appropriate manner, when recognizing the emotions of others.

And as the child progresses:

16. Child will retell a story or answer questions about what he has read, to include character, setting and main events in sequence.

17. Child will learn to give spontaneous compliments.

18. Child will give appropriate verbal feedback in conversation, including comments and rejoinder questions.

19. Child will ask for help, clarification or repetition if he doesn't understand or remember what is said.

20. Child will follow instructions that require math vocabulary: more, fewer, less than.

21. Child will describe how two events, objects or people are alike and how they are different. *Tip:* Use subject matter relevant to the child to teach concepts. If Sam is a movie lover, ask him to compare how *Shrek* and *Shrek 2* are alike and how they are different.

22. Child will describe why he does or doesn't like a story.

23. Child will understand and accurately use ten homonyms (antonyms, synonyms) from his reading material.

24. Child will understand ten common idioms.

25. Child will use irregular past tense verbs accurately (ate instead of eated, drew instead of drawed, rode instead of rided).

Jump-starting literacy for concrete thinkers. You may have discovered that perennial childhood favorites like Peter Rabbit or Winnie the Pooh get no response from your young one. Stories that revolve around animals who not only talk, but wear clothes, drive cars and keep house can be incomprehensible and disturbing for children with autism. When typical children's literature doesn't make sense, a different approach is required.

Because children with ASD are very visually oriented and often language-challenged, concentrate on choosing books with these characteristics:

- Books with photographs, not drawn illustrations.
- Books about real-life things that a child can correlate with his own life, such as construction equipment, babies, ice cream, farms, the zoo or parks.
- Books about people (especially children), not animals, and certainly not animals with anthropomorphic tendencies.
- Books about the child himself: Window books have a cutout in each page. Tape your child's photo to the back page of the book and his/her face appears on every page. Try the *Hey, Look at Me!* series from Merrybooks. Or create your own book, using family photos as illustrations. Write about a past event ("My 5th Birthday Party") or a familiar routine ("Thanksgiving at My Grandma's House").

Scout the library's nonfiction section for fact-based books with strong photographs about things that are interesting to the child. There are literally thousands of photo-essay books for kids. Here are just a few:

- Scholastic's *Let's Find Out* series: big, bright photographs of kids learning about things like bicycles, toothpaste and money.
- Dorling-Kindersley Books (DK) offers literally thousands of nonfiction titles. *Jobs People Do* features children in grown-up attire as doctors, fishermen, photographers, chefs, etc. A

related series: *A Day in the Life* of . . . *a Dancer, Police Officer, Lifeguard*, etc.

- Baby animals may intrigue. DK's series *See How They Grow* acquaints kids with Puppy, Kitten, Foal, Duck, Lamb, Chick, and many more. Compass Point Books' *Animals and Their Young* series has titles like *Bears Have Cubs, Pigs Have Piglets, Cows Have Calves.*

- Tana Hoban's dozens of photo-illustrated books introduce children to many concepts around them, such as *Colors Everywhere, Is It Rough? Is It Smooth?, Shadows and Reflections.*

- *From Wheat to Pasta, From Plant to Blue Jeans* and *From Wax to Crayon* are representative of photo-essay titles from the Changes series published by New York Children's Press.

- *Our Neighborhood* is a people-based series including *The Zieglers and their Apple Orchard, Exploring Parks with Ranger Dockett, Learning about Bees with Mr. Krebs.*

- Mr. Rogers books cover many potentially difficult situations, from "first experiences" (*The New Baby, Going to the Doctor, Making Friends*) to tough transitions (*Moving, When a Pet Dies, Divorce*).

- For the 3rd to 5th grade child, The Grandmothers at Work series is irresistible. *Meet My Grandmother: She's a United States Senator* as told by Dianne Feinstein's six-year-old granddaughter: "When a bill Gagi has written gets passed . . . Gagi goes to a meeting with the President." Equally charming is *Meet My Grandmother: She's a Supreme Court Justice* as told by Sandra Day O'Connor's granddaughter.

Once the connection to books is made, keep the momentum going:

- When you find a book that works for your child, exhaust the series, the author, the genre.

- If a favorite among the library books emerges—buy it. Nothing is more discouraging to a budding reader than to discover his beloved new "friend" has been returned.

- Don't waste energy bemoaning that young Peyton doesn't like Frog and Toad even though you did. With time and acclimation, that may change. It's a short leap from reading about construction equipment to reading *Mike Mulligan and His Steam Shovel.*

Blueprint his work. You can help a child communicate her process (whether drawing, writing, or creating or accomplishing a physical goal) by documenting it through words and drawings by either you or the child. Eight-year-old Jamie had put together a block ramp much like the other children were putting together, but with fewer blocks. Before it was taken apart and put away, his paraeducator drew the way the blocks had been put together on a piece of paper, and had Jamie write about it. Jamie wrote: "The ramp is a tunnel ramp. The two trucks don't fit in the tunnel ramp." He tried to build it taller, but time ran out, and the activity ended for the day. The drawings were a "blueprint" for being able to come back to the activity another day and try again. Also, a copy could be sent home to Mom and Dad to keep them updated on Jamie's school projects for the day.

Crossword fun. So easy to do! Visit this great website www.crosswordpuzzlegames.com/create.html to create a crossword puzzle tailored for your child. You make up the words and the clues, so it will always be at his ability level. High interest is guaranteed when you use words that pertain to his interests, his family members, his experiences. Create a small book of puzzles as an extra-special gift for your child or student.

The talking stick. Talking in a group, even informally, can be an anxiety-laden activity for kids with ASD. Knowing when to talk, what to say and how to say it involves not just speech, but complex mental processing. Reduce some of that anxiety by using a brightly colored object, passed from child to child, as a visual indication of whose turn it is to speak.

Night and day. Temporal concepts (references to time) are difficult for many children with ASD. To help your child or student, relate temporal terms to familiar activities and verbalize them frequently. *Morning* is the time we eat breakfast. *Nighttime* is when it is dark outside and we get ready for bed. In the *summer* it is hot and we don't go to school. In the *winter* it's cold and we wear coats and mittens.

Chapter 3

Strong Reasons

Behavior Strategies and Considerations

Strong reasons make strong actions.

William Shakespeare

Ideas to live by. Behavior is communication. We repeat: Behavior is communication. All behavior, whether appropriate or inappropriate, is a message about how a child perceives what is happening around him or her. Inappropriate or negative behaviors interfere with a child's learning process whether at school, at home or in social situations. Extinguishing these behaviors is not enough; *exchanging* these behaviors with appropriate alternatives that fulfill the same function as the original behavior has to happen so that real learning can flow.

Most autism professionals and educators will tell you that your child or student truly does want to interact appropriately with people and the world around him. When inappropriate behavior occurs, it is generally because the child is overwhelmed by disordered sensory systems, cannot communicate his wants or needs or doesn't understand the situation or what is expected of him.

As you approach any behavior incident or situation involving a child with ASD, keep in mind the following five guidelines:

Look for sensory issues.

Resistant behaviors can have their root in sensory issues.

Look beyond the behavior to find the source of the resistance.

Never assume anything.

He may not know or understand the rules.

She may have heard the instructions but not understood them.

Maybe he knew it yesterday but has forgotten it today.

She cannot comply if she doesn't comprehend.

Teach functional communication.

Without a functional communication system of some sort, expect behavior problems.

This especially applies to children who are nonverbal or with very limited verbal skills.

They still need a way to express their wants and needs.

Behavior occurs for a reason.

It may be to get attention, to get a need met, or to avoid doing something.

When working to change an inappropriate behavior, we must recognize that the underlying need that spurred the behavior in the first place still exists.

It's important to provide an appropriate substitute behavior that will meet that same need. Otherwise, why should a child give up the behavior? Just because you want him to?

Watch what you reinforce.

Even well-intentioned parents and professionals can unknowingly reinforce the very behavior they're working to change in a child. Periodically do a reality check of your own behavior when you find your behavior methods not working.

Not just for baseball anymore. Ever notice how baseball coaches communicate with their batters and runners through a series of hand signals? Develop a similar set of discreet cues to let your child know when a behavior is inappropriate. Putting a finger on your chin might mean, "You are interrupting." Lacing your fingers together might mean, "You are monopolizing the conversation; let someone else talk now."

Accentuate the positive. Think through your responses to inappropriate behavior to ensure that 1) you are modeling appropriate behavior and 2) you are not unwittingly encouraging further negative behavior. A child may respond to "punishment" by lying, cheating or trying to shift blame to someone else. A willful child may also "win" this game by developing a tolerance to the penalty. What, then? Do you escalate the penalty? If you do, where does it end?

A better overall approach is to constantly encourage appropriate behaviors and interactions, no matter how small the increment. Discuss infractions at a time when both you and she are calm, not at the height of the battle.

A change of view. To break perseverative behavior, change the scenery. Send the child on an errand; walk to the office, the rest room, the mailbox, the back yard.

Vanquish a dangerous behavior by constructing a visual barrier. Teachers in a classroom that was half below ground had a problem with a child continually jumping from the wide window sill that was placed at ground level. His art-savvy paraeducator stopped the behavior by creating a mural on the lower wall of an earth to sky, then disguised the ledge with "clouds." End of behavior. Challenging behaviors sometimes require creative solutions.

Fear of bathroom = fear of the dark. One little boy with whom our paraeducator worked would not use the restroom at school. The restroom was windowless, and the child was eventually able to tell teachers that some students had teased him by turning off the lights while he was in there, leaving him alone in the pitch dark. The solution: providing him with a large flashlight that could be set on the floor inside the stall. The flashlight was stored in his cubby. The child was resourceful enough to come up with a reply to students who asked why he took a flashlight into the restroom: "In case the power goes off!"

Time-shifting: not just for grown-ups. If certain tasks or outings are met with resistance, consider that it may be the time of day rather than the actual task. You yourself do not enjoy having to perform chores when you are tired, hungry or want to watch your favorite show. Reschedule unloved tasks to other times of day. An unwanted haircut will not go smoothly right before nap time, but right after might work. His teeth will be just as clean if he brushes them right after dinner than if he waits until bedtime. Use a "first-then" tactic for boring chores: First, we put our toys away, then we watch Reading Rainbow.

Resistant/avoidant behavior. This is one area wherein an ounce of prevention is worth a pound of cure. Resistant/avoidant behaviors strain even the most patient of parents and teachers, but remember your guidelines—behavior is communication; assume *nothing*—and proceed with these tactics:

- Identify the source: Keep a journal noting what happened or was happening immediately before the meltdown. Note people involved, time of day, activities, settings, sensory issues. Over time a pattern may emerge. If you can identify the antecedent (i.e., the trigger) to the behavior, you can avoid, eliminate or address it.

- Phrase requests in the positive rather than the imperative. "You are tracking mud all over the house!" may provoke a stubborn refusal to remove shoes. A cheery "Please park your shoes by the back door" may be met with more cooperation. Plus, there will be situations when your very literal ASD child may not understand the action your imperative implies. To him, you're simply stating the obvious. Inferring that you want him to alter his behavior may be beyond his social-cognitive thinking. Verbalizing the behavior in the positive form clearly vocalizes your request and at the same time reinforces appropriate behavior. It removes the guessing game of the child having to figure out what he should do.

- Does the child really know how to do what is being asked of him? If he suddenly needs to run to the bathroom every time he's asked to set the table or do a math sheet, maybe he doesn't know how or fears his effort will not be good enough and draw criticism. Stick with him through enough repetitions of the task to where he feels competent. Most kids with ASD will need more practice to master tasks than will their NT counterparts. Show patience.

- Does the child actually know the rules? Does he understand the reason for the rule (safety, economy, health, etc.)? Is he breaking the well-known rule because there might be an underlying cause? Maybe he is pinching forbidden snacks out of the fridge because he was worried about finishing his art project, didn't eat his lunch and is now famished. (Establishing a communication check-in each day with your child's teacher or assistant is helpful in avoiding such incidents. The teacher would have reported that he didn't eat his lunch.)

- Provide a breather, a break to allow for self-regulation *before* the behavior gets out of hand. This should feel like a positive regrouping time, not jail. Sending the child to her room or the hallway may be too far physically removed to allow smooth reintegration to the activity flow of home or classroom. Furthermore, this should not be viewed as punishment or a consequence for inappropriate behavior. The purpose of the breather is to encourage self-regulation. At a time when she is calm, pre-designate a spot she can go to for a few minutes when she is overwhelmed and feels she can't or doesn't want to cooperate. *Ask her* what items might be good for this spot. A favorite book or plush animal, pillow or chair, headphones with favorite music?

- Keep your behavioral expectations reasonable and age-appropriate. Church services, restaurants, concerts or other events requiring long quiet sits are set-ups for conflict. Arrange movement breaks at reasonable intervals, or abbreviate or skip the activity until she is older and better able to handle it.

- Timing is everything. Of course he would rather play with his cars than go to pick up his sister at dance practice, but a little respect goes a long way. Give him a five-minute warning and a two-minute warning—and build a few extra minutes in on your end to compensate for resistance or dawdling. This holds true for asking him to interrupt any pleasurable activity (play, TV or reading) in order to perform a less pleasurable one (chores, errands or unwanted appointments).

- If nagging has become the norm in your house, you've probably noticed that it is ineffective and irritating to all parties. *Ask your child* to help you think of better ways to accomplish what needs to get done. Depending on his age and ability, he may or may not be able to verbalize suggestions but you will have given him the respect and the opportunity to be part of the solution. If he can verbalize he may tell you that when he gets home from school he likes to run around the backyard for a while before settling down to homework, or that the toothpaste you've been buying tastes horrible to him so he avoids brushing his teeth.

- Set up visual schedules and charts that you can discreetly point to as gentle reminders of what he needs to do. Children with ASD are visual learners; his auditory channel may shut down in times of stress. Your child can refer to these visuals as concrete reminders of what he should do, especially when anger or irritation is creeping in. Your goal is for your child to independently act in appropriate ways, without using you as a crutch to guide his every action.

- Reality check: Is your love for your child "user-friendly" or does it feel conditional? If the vibes she picks up tell her that your love depends on a tidy room, good grades or perfect behavior, she may feel defeated enough to not even try.

Hostile or aggressive behavior: hitting, biting, scratching, shoving. These tough and sometimes baffling behaviors may erupt out of seemingly nowhere, or may be wearyingly ongoing. Meeting them with logic rather than emotion is surely difficult—and surely worth it. You can make major headway if you:

- First, understand where the behavior is coming from. Almost all such behaviors are rooted in your child's sensory and/or social impairments. He is not doing it to provoke you, embarrass you or make your life miserable. He is not an inherently unkind, cruel, malicious or evil individual. He is most likely feeling frustrated, fearful, threatened, tired, unable to communicate his needs or otherwise unable to cope. Let your response spring from this understanding.

- Respond at the first infraction. Don't wait until the third or fourth time he's swung a fist to see if "he figures it out" from the other child's reaction. He needs a crystal-clear directive from you that such behavior is not acceptable.

- Respond in the same manner every time, in word, action and consequence. It may take many repetitions to imprint and the consistency aids in comprehension.

- *Do not* respond in kind. You are trying to get him to change an inappropriate behavior and you must lead by example. Answering aggression with aggression (yelling, spanking) will only confuse him hopelessly in ways he cannot possibly process: it's not okay to hit other children, but is it okay to be aggressive if you are the bigger person? The horrifying long-term consequence of this is that he may not tell you if, in the future, another adult behaves aggressively or abusively toward him.

- Impose natural consequences, not "punishment." Punitive punishment for noncompliance or inappropriate behavior will almost certainly be ineffective in the long run. Without an understanding of cause and effect, your intent will be lost on your child and succeed only in lowering his self-esteem without any understanding of what to do differently next time. Focus on helping him understand the natural consequences of his actions: If you hit Bryan, he will not want to play with you. If you leave your truck in the hallway, it will get stepped on, broken, and you will not have it to play with anymore. At the same time, offer positive reinforcement for compliance and appropriate behaviors. Additional strategies:

    ~ Restitution: "Tommy's crayons are broken. You'll need to give him some of yours (or buy him a new box)."

    ~ Emotional awareness: "I know you didn't mean to hurt Kelly (or, hurt Kelly's feelings/make Kelly feel bad). Let's say I'm sorry."

- Evaluate where aggressive messages are coming from in his life. Children with autism are famous for concrete thinking, and your child may have great difficulty distinguishing fantasy from reality. It may be worth weaning him off television programs and computer games that portray such behavior in entertaining or unrealistic ways.

~ Know what your child is watching or playing—watch or play it with him.

~ If you do decide to ban a show or game, taking it away cold turkey may or may not be the easiest way. Gradually reducing the time allowed may ease the transition: Week one: He may play Cosmic Combat for thirty minutes. Week two: reduce time to twenty or twenty-five minutes. Week three and beyond: continue reducing time allowed until it is eliminated. You can also gradually reduce the number of days on which he is allowed to play it: every other day, every third day, etc. until eliminated.

~ *To be upfront about it or not?* Your call—your child. If you gradually reduce time, will he notice? Or will he be better off if you are straightforward in your explanation: "This program/game shows people being hurtful to each other. This is not okay and we are not going to watch it/play it."

~ Offer substitute programs or games. Respect his feelings in doing so—offer replacement activities that will truly interest him, not just lame time-fillers. (These may take a bit of homework on your part to find.)

• Praise appropriate social behavior and do it often. Just as he does not hit out of innate nastiness, neither may he understand that waiting his turn (and other examples of self-control) is good.

Studies by George Gerbner, Ph.D., at the University of Pennsylvania, have shown that children's TV shows contain about twenty violent acts each hour and also that children who watch a lot of television are more likely to think that the world is a mean and dangerous place. Source: http://www.apa.org/pubinfo/violence.html

Tantrums and meltdowns: guidelines for adults. A child or student's meltdown is a stressful experience for everyone involved. Having a working plan put together ahead of time can alleviate some of the stress and allow you to respond in as calm a manner as possible.

To follow are six simple guidelines for effective behavior management during a tantrum or meltdown. Try them and you'll find that the tantrum is over a lot quicker and is easier on everyone.

1. Don't try to teach during a tantrum—it is rarely successful.

2. The more stressed the situation, the more reduced and concrete your language should be.

3. Set a rule that once a situation gets out of hand, one previously designated person provides direction and input. Everyone talking at the same time will just escalate the situation for the child.

4. Rehearse your behavior plan ahead of time. Many plans that look good on paper are just not effective in practice.

5. Time-outs are good —for both of you. When your child has danced on your third nerve for the tenth time since lunch, don't blow. Tell her: "I am very angry right now and I can't be around you. I am going to my room to calm down for a few minutes, then I will come back and we will talk about it." Modeling this sort of self-control will help your child begin to understand how she can manage her own behavior too.

6. Choose only battles with significant consequences. Yes, she must wear her seat belt in the car and she must wear a helmet when riding her bike. But are books on the shelf upside down really an issue? Establish a list of nonnegotiable "have-to" items (taking her medicine, going to school, wearing sunscreen at the beach, the afore-mentioned seat belts and bike helmets) and be as flexible and creative as you can about everything else.

Peer power and the two-minute warning. Giving the child a "two-minute warning" when an activity is about to change is a good behavior practice. If he is resistant or reluctant, try getting a peer to help him. Peers often have more suggestive power than adults do.

Photo-reinforcer. Cut up a photo of a favorite reinforcer to use with a token system, e.g., a photo of a computer for computer time, or the cover of a favorite video. When first using the token system, or with a particularly difficult task, cut the photo into a small number of pieces. The idea is to foster success, not make the token system so difficult that the child loses interest. As skills build, cut the photo into a larger number of pieces. To avoid the child feeling like you're cheating by making it harder and harder to get the reward (delayed gratification), try using a slightly different photo each time.

Flexibility required alert. Congratulations! By learning to consult his visual schedule, your child or student has achieved some measure of independence in getting through his day. However, change is a certainty of life, and teaching our kids how to accept change and avoid rigidity in thought and behavior is a skill that will benefit them throughout their lives.

- When there is going to be a blip in the usual routine, give him fair warning with a red frame around the particular event that is different that day—school assembly, doctor appointment instead of coming straight home. He has a better chance of integrating it smoothly into his day if it is not a surprise.

- Remember to consider his routine from two standpoints. He needs to know not only what is going to happen that day that is different, but also what *isn't* going to happen that day that usually does.

- Increase behavioral flexibility and your child's tolerance to change by inserting a question mark (?) on her daily schedule from time to time. At first, it should represent something that will be enjoyable to the child: a new way to play a game, a surprise snack, or a special outing at school. Gradually introduce less desirable events or conditions as the child becomes more able to tolerate changes. Building mystery into the routine helps kids become more adaptable when real surprises and changes occur in daily life.

Mirror, mirror on the wall? If your child has a fascination with looking at himself, make it work for you. Take a camera with you wherever you go, and snap pictures of your child in different settings. Arrange them in a colorful scrapbook, so he can see himself at these places. Helping your child recall pleasant times can decrease anxiety about returning to these environments, or going to new, different places.

Helping a self-biter. The child who bites himself in frustration is surely one of the more alarming classroom challenges. Conducting a functional behavior analysis to determine the antecedent to the behavior will help you take steps to prevent it. In the school setting, have staff observe the child throughout the day to pinpoint and record the times he bites himself. Is it circle time, one-on-one work time with his assistant, transition times? Does it occur when a certain person is present, when the noise levels are elevated, just after lunch or always during art?

Effective measures to reduce the biting will vary from child to child. But here's a simple idea worth trying out. Give the child a rather large wad of gum to chew at these times, equivalent to two or three sticks. Many OTs have found that the deep proprioceptive oral input of the chewing calms the child to where the biting ceases. Jerky, fruit leather, other chewy foods or nontoxic objects may also help. Our OT uses pen suspenders from www.pdppro.com. They are a soft plastic pen holder on a neckcord the child can keep with him for anytime chomping. Or put a piece of aquarium tubing (available at pet stores) on the end of his pencil.

> *Tip*: We're saying it again, but many negative behaviors are rooted in sensory dysfunction, meaning the child is receiving some sort of sensory input from the biting

beyond just the expression of frustration or anger. Attempting to merely interrupt the behavior ("No!") when it occurs without addressing the root cause will ultimately be ineffective. If the child is truly seeking proprioceptive feedback he may merely shift from biting to a similar self-destructive behavior (hair-pulling, nail biting, etc.). In the interim, put something over the portion of his body that he is biting: glove, long sleeve shirt, ace bandage.

Note: Collar- and cuff-chewers are a subset of self-biters. The same tactics can be used.

A thought: Edible necklaces can be an **occasional short-term solution**, perhaps for a car ride, doctor's office wait or other non-daily stress. They can be made from string licorice threaded with any hole-in-the-middle cereal or candy (Cheerios®, LifeSavers®). We don't recommend regular usage because they are nutritionally awful, loaded with dyes, sugars and possible allergens. As always, weigh the tradeoffs of each situation. If it gets you through that forty-minute plane trip without the screaming, it might be worth a little hyper behavior on the other end. Or not. (Smile.)

Please remain seated. Children who have trouble remaining seated on the floor or in their chairs may be coping with several things ranging from poor postural control to vestibular or motor planning problems. Defining their seating area in more obvious ways may help.

- A strip of foam pipe insulation (the kind that is pre-slit to slip over the pipe) applied to the edge of his chair; that raised edge may do the trick
- A chair cushion or camp pillow
- A carpet square
- Tape around his spot on the floor

The gentle way to criticize. Let's be honest, who among us likes to listen to criticism, however "constructive"? Accepting criticism is a life skill demanding maturity and a certain amount of self-confidence that may be light years beyond your child's abilities right now. Should you never correct a hyper-sensitive child? Of course not. But it's all in the delivery.

- First, foremost and forever: never, *ever* try to impose discipline, correction or disapproval when the child is in the middle of a meltdown, shutdown, anxiety episode or any other emotional state rendering her unable to interact with you.

- Before you even speak, remember that your very sensory-challenged, language-impaired child will react as much, if not more, to the qualities of your voice than to the actual words. She will hear the yelling, the derision, the rhetorical sarcasm, the hysterical pitch, but she will not understand the words and therefore will not be able to figure out what she did wrong. Speak in low tones, and if possible, lower your body as well, so that you are communicating on her level rather than towering over her.

- Adopt a "social autopsy" approach:

    ~ Identify the behavior and handle it in a supportive, problem-solving manner rather than invoking punishment or other negative consequences.

    Note: Your child may need help pinning down the feelings that triggered the behavior. He may say he was angry when in fact he may have been afraid, frustrated, sad, overexcited or jealous. Probe beyond his first response.

    ~ Practice or role-play a better way to handle the situation next time it occurs, actively involving the child in the solution.

    ~ Conduct the "autopsy" as soon after the incident as possible.

~ Expect to drill or role-play over time. There are no one-time fixes.

~ Provide immediate positive feedback for future episodes when she gets it right.

- Present the information visually through a storyboard, comic strip, photo essay or social story.

- Ensure that you yourself are modeling proper behavior for responding to criticism.

When stubborn behaviors persist. Reinforcement is a powerful teaching tool at school or at home. When used correctly, great things can happen. However, be aware that it's extremely easy to inadvertently reinforce the very behavior you're trying to extinguish. An example: Johnny doesn't enjoy morning Circle Time at his preschool program and often runs out of the circle over to the art easel and starts to draw. Knowing that Johnny loves goldfish crackers, the teacher decides to use them as their ending snack. As she starts sharing them with the other students, back comes Johnny, plopping himself down as the crackers make their way to his spot. The teacher responds to him "Nice sitting in group Johnny", thinking she is reinforcing the appropriate behavior he is now exhibiting, and gives him some crackers. She should think again. Johnny didn't sit nicely in group; he ran out of the circle and only returned when something interested him. But he still got the reinforcement along with the other children. What the teacher wanted to teach him was to stay with the group during Circle Time. What she actually reinforced was that he could get up and run away and still get the reward.

Avoid this common error by making sure that reinforcers follow performance and are specific to the performance desired. If the teacher had asked Johnny to **do** something when he got back to the circle or required him to wait for the next cracker delivery he might have learned the lesson she was trying to teach.

Real choices. Another common teaching blooper is the "Do you want—?" question, especially with individuals with ASD, who are literal in their listening and responses. "Do you want to go to lunch?", "Do you want to do your homework now?" We often pose a question to a child when in reality, there is no choice being offered. The result is that we teach a child that we are untrustworthy in our actions, or that choices only happen sometimes or really not at all. The solution is simple. Don't offer a choice or ask that "Do you want—?" question unless you mean it and are willing to accept no for an answer. "No" is one of the acceptable answers to "Do you want—?"

Think ahead. If your child's object of intense interest is seasonal, and if playing off that interest is going to be key in motivating behavior and/or routine, make it a point to think ahead and stock up on related items at the appropriate time. Does he love Halloween? Stock up on stickers for his visual chart, paper napkins for his lunchbox, fake cobwebs for his room, etc. Is she a water baby? Snorkels, goggles and float toys are fun in the bathtub, hot tub and indoor pool all year 'round, but you'd better buy them in the summer if you want a plentiful selection. If your young paleontologist is going to want a dinosaur egg hunt at his birthday party in September, better buy the plastic Easter eggs in the spring.

Secret knock. Barging into a sibling's room or bathroom without knocking can be infuriating to the sibling; it is equally unacceptable in other people's homes or in a business setting. Have the two siblings develop a secret knock that must be used to enter each other's rooms. (Emphasize "secret knock, then wait for Julie to say, 'come in.'") Tell the NT sibling to practice it at odd times, even if it's only to check in and say hello. Give the autism sibling positive reinforcement each time he uses the secret knock—a piece of gum or token that can be used toward something he likes.

Deals and contracts. Contracts and deals can be effective behavior management tools with kids with ASD, both at home or in the classroom environment. We already use them informally: "Pick up your room and you can go to the movies." "Finish your math and you can watch that TV program." More formal systems include point systems and token earning systems.

When used effectively, deals and contracts can reduce behavioral problems, keep attention focused, and help teach one of life's critical lessons: work = reward. However, pitfalls and traps abound in setting up contracts and deals, especially with individuals with ASD who often lack important social skills that contribute to a shared understanding of the contract's parameters. Adhere to these simple but important guidelines for setting up contacts and deals.

- Whenever possible, make the contract visual. It can be simple pictures or symbols or a formal, written document. Try using a "Working for ___" card (i.e., tangible reward like candy or a favorite toy or activity). The card can be just a picture of the reward with a space to write in steps to achieve the reward. Start simple, with just a few steps, or maybe even one. We want the child to start with success and build from there.

- Contract rules need to be clear and concise. Individuals with autism think in a very literal manner. Use straightforward terms that can be clearly evaluated by both parties involved.

- Check for comprehension. Unless you are 100% certain that the student understands what is expected of him, the timelines of the contract, and the reward, don't institute the contract. Go back and simplify or adjust the terms of the contract.

- Honor the deal. This is one of the biggest mistakes that well-meaning parents and professionals regularly make. Contracts involve at least two people, and each person has a defined part in the deal. I do this; you do that. These rules are accepted as part of the agreement and govern the interaction. If one party 'breaks the rules', trust is immediately broken and often a behavior problem develops. An example: A teacher and student made a contract, but when the teacher changed the rules in midstream, the student revolted. "He finished the work before the period was over, so I asked him to do some more work. He became upset." Note the key word "finished." The student fulfilled his end of the contract; he did what he was asked to do. However, the teacher broke the deal. Who wouldn't resist? The fact that the student finished ahead of time was a planning problem, not a behavioral problem. Next time the teacher might make the contract a little tighter or include more work for the reward. It's much easier to revamp a subsequent contract than to rebuild trust in a relationship after it is broken. Once you've set up a deal, stick to it!

- Be thorough. Think about the many contracts and deals in your life. Most include the basics: how much work we have to do, what behaviors or actions are expected of us, what reward we'll receive and when we get paid. We need to include all of these elements in our contracts with kids, too.

- Start small and expand gradually. If you're just introducing contracts or deals to a child, make the terms simple. One piece of work equals one payoff or reward. Don't get anxious and raise the stakes too quickly. Remember: Each time the child is successful you have reinforced work and the child has had an opportunity to practice effective social interaction. Those are good things to do!

- Avoid setting yourself—and the child—up for failure. Make sure the end result or actions specified in the contract are attainable by the child. Add time or work amounts slowly. And don't forget that these contracts play out in real life. We often have bad days at work and we still get paid. Consider having alternate reinforcers available if the contract doesn't get fulfilled.

- Make "payday or payoff" reasonable. The timeline for the contract has to be within the student's ability right from the start. If the payoff is too far in the future, motivation will slip. Even worse, we may find that behavioral problems develop.

- Watch out for "blackmail." If you find yourself saying "If you stop your tantrum you'll get _____", you are setting yourself up for trouble. You are now teaching the child that he can get paid to stop behaving in a certain way. What happens after that? The child makes you raise the ante before he stops misbehaving and the time interval between paydays gets shorter and shorter. That's not a direction in which you want to go.

- Watch out for sloppy and imprecise language. "If you're good, you'll get_____." "Good" is subjective; it can change from day to day and person to person. Terms like this in a contract can be very confusing to a person with ASD.

- Refrain from using rewards that are so big or important to the person that losing them (or the anxiety caused by thinking they might not be attained) will be too stressful for the child to handle. We want to encourage progress, not add undue stress to the experience.

From bad to worse: how to avoid escalating a skirmish.

We are all human and despite our supposed adult maturity, we sometimes make bad decisions in the heat of the moment. An ASD child in full meltdown is surely an unhappy situation for any classroom, but teachers (and parents at home) can do much to ensure that they are not prolonging the episode by responding with inflammatory behavior of their own. Beware of specific behaviors that further rather than resolve a crisis:

- Raising pitch or volume of voice (yelling, shrieking)
- Presenting threatening body language, such as clenched fists, narrowed eyes, towering or advancing posture
- Mocking or mimicking the student, using sarcasm, insults or humiliating remarks, attempting to embarrass the student out of the behavior
- Attacking the student's character or personality
- Making unsubstantiated accusations
- Rewarding unacceptable behavior, bribing
- Nagging or preaching
- Invoking a double standard
- Comparing student to sibling or other student

- Referencing previous or unrelated events

- Lumping the child into a general category (kids like her are "all the same")

- Making an assumption—any kind of assumption—without factual backup, i.e., you may have given him an instruction, but that doesn't mean he was able to understand it.

Chapter 4

To Do and Understand

Daily Living Strategies and Considerations

I hear and I forget. I see and I remember. I do and I understand.

Confucius

Movin' on to a new home. The move to a new home can present a towering challenge to the child with autism, particularly if the move involves not only a new house or apartment, but a new school and/or a new town as well. This is an overwhelming amount of change for a child who cherishes sameness and routine. But there are many things you can do to ease the transition.

- First and most important: Take your child's special needs into consideration when choosing the home. If he is noise sensitive, don't locate near a subway, stadium/concert venue, raceway, factory, etc. Stand in different parts of the home and the yard and listen carefully. Noise can carry for several miles under certain weather conditions, and what may not be immediately noticeable to you may be unbearable for him. Does your child tantrum or melt down frequently? Choose that apartment very carefully—ground floor, end unit.

- Be sensitive to how you are phrasing your descriptions of the move. If the term "new house" seems to trouble him, call it another house, a different house, a blue house, our next house. Same goes with all the other "new" things that will happen.

- Ensure that he understands that all family members, not just him, are making the move and that *all* of his stuff is going with him, unlike vacation where some things are left behind. Also be clear that neighbors, and friends as it applies, will not be coming along.

- Knowledge is power. The more he knows about his next home or school, the more familiar it will seem to him. Reporters are trained to think in terms of the five "W" questions: what, when, where, who and why (with "how" thrown in for good measure). News stories are constructed in pyramid fashion, with the broadest and most important information coming first. More and more detail is added as the reader or listener's attention allows. This is a good way to think of presenting information about your move to your child. He can then acclimate to the information at his own pace rather than being drowned by a tsunami of facts and information.

• As your child gains more facts, help him write a story comparing and contrasting the differences between the environment you are leaving and the one to which you are going: these things about my family will not change/will be the same, and these things will be different. Emphasize "what's in it for him" at the new location. Does the new town have an aquarium, a state-of-the-art movie theatre or library, a public swimming pool nearby? Does the new house have a bigger yard, a sidewalk for riding his scooter, an eating bar in the kitchen, a cool fireplace for roasting marshmallows?

• Provide photographs of the house from as many angles as possible, and do drive-bys, if possible. After the previous owners have moved, take photos of the rooms inside and back yard. (Photos depicting previous owners' belongings may be confusing or set up false expectations.)

• Will your child have his own room, and will he be allowed to choose new accoutrements such as carpet or paint? Providing carpet square samples and paint chips from which to choose gives him some control over his new environment. It should go without saying, but we'll say it anyway: Give him only samples and colors that are within your budget and your willingness to execute. Don't give him a sample of carpet that is going to illicit a "we can't afford that one" response, and don't give him a palette of paint chips in the orange category if you are truly not going to be able to tolerate looking at orange every day. Or, if you can tolerate the lighter shades but not the darker ones, cut the darker end of the chip strip off before giving it to him.

Off-gassing: A Word of Warning About New Carpets and Floors

(and drapes, blinds, paneling and shower curtains)

If your child is chemically sensitive, be aware that new carpeting and flooring may off-gas literally dozens of chemicals that may make your child ill, at least temporarily. Formaldehyde, ethylbenzene, toluene, xylene, styrene, benzene and a host of other substances are used to manufacture synthetic carpetings and floorings, their backings, the glues that attach them to subfloors and the stain-proofing/moth-proofing applied to them. Indications of sensitivity include eye, nose and throat irritation, cough, flu-like symptoms, headache, dizziness or disorientation, overall malaise.

If possible, install new carpeting, paint and window coverings in your new home several weeks before moving, and keep windows open as much as possible in the interim. Look through "alternative materials" books and catalogs for low-chemical paints, stains and floor sealants that are available. And remember, the more energy-efficient the home, the harder it is for trapped gasses to escape.

Or consider installing natural-material hard surface flooring such as bamboo, tile, cork or wood (with minimal chemical stain). Natural-fiber area rugs can provide warmth, texture, color and comfort.

Green houseplants can also help, assuming spore and mold allergies are not an issue.

- If the new school is in a distant town, send a disposable camera along with a postage-paid self-addressed return envelope to the school secretary, resource teacher or other willing staff member. Ask that they envision your child's day and take pictures of those things: the classroom and teacher, the hallway, the cafeteria and head cook, the gym and PE teacher, the library and librarian, the playground (preferably during recess with kids on the equipment), the music room and music teacher, the principal and office staff, the resource room. Specifically include any items that are of special interest to him: art supplies, science books, medicine balls.

- Upon arriving at the new house, set up his bedroom before anything else so he can see that his bed, his books, his computer and his toys are all there. If your move is local, try to accomplish this while he is away at school so that he comes home to a room that is not in chaos, even if the rest of the house is.

- Follow up with a visit to the old house in its empty-shell condition, so he can see that all his stuff is at the new house.

- Be clear about household rules that have followed you to the new house (no shoes in the living room, no food outside the kitchen) as well as any rules that are new to the new house (no jumping off the stairs when moving from a one-story to a two-story house). A visual chart may help.

- Maintain as much consistency as possible. Can you shop at the same supermarket, or one that looks just like it? Can he continue with the same karate teacher? Will the family pet be making the move too? Can the old winter coat last one more year? Breakfast should look the same and so should bedtime.

- When you find yourself expressing the inevitable anger or frustration at the foibles of moving, take a minute to ensure that he knows it's not his fault. Whether they are verbal or nonverbal, children intuit a great deal more than we realize.

- Allow him to acclimate to the new house in his own time and in his own way. It not only looks different to him, it smells different, it sounds different and it requires different navigation skills. He may stick to his room for the first few days or even weeks, but eventually you will be able to help him explore. Giving him a specific job that requires him to come out of his room each day may help: feeding Snowball, putting his clothes in the laundry room or watering the houseplants (break into groups so he does a few each day).

Go ahead—scribble on the wall. She's going to do it anyway, so why not give her a legitimate "canvas." Paint one (untextured) wall of her room, playroom, kitchen or other suitable location with chalkboard/blackboard paint. If you don't have a whole wall to spare, use the spray paint version to cover a tabletop, floor area or other flat surface.

Any-holiday cheer. Help a child weave plaid, satin or any novelty ribbon through the upper holes of pretzels twists for a charming garland for the mantle, door or holiday tree. After the holiday, drape it around an outdoor tree for the birds.

Easing separation anxiety. If your child experiences separation anxiety, use her super-sensitive sense of smell to help. Place a drop of your perfume, shampoo or other familiar-scented item inside the collar of her shirt. She can take a sniff any time during the day to feel connected to you. Or, let her wear a T-shirt or sweater that you have worn, which will also have a personal scent clinging to it. Other ideas for easing separation anxiety:

- Create a small photo album depicting your child's day: waking up, eating breakfast, getting on the bus, various activities during the school day, coming home to Mom, dinner, bedtime. She can keep the photo album in her cubby or backpack and refer to it when she feels anxious.

- If your child has a favorite story character, talk about how he or she might handle being away at school. What would Grover do? Maybe he would make a list of all the fun things he does at school. Maybe he would think about other brave things he had done, like jumping off the diving board or riding the bus or sleeping in the bunk bed.

- A locket or other photo necklace around her neck is something she can pull out during the day for visual reassurance.

- Make breakfast a "have-to" each morning. Anxiety is more pronounced in children who are hungry, tired, sick or otherwise stressed.

Tip: Anything nutritious is a "breakfast food." Pizza, pork chops, spaghetti and peanut butter are just as suitable at 7:00 am as they are at 7:00 pm. His stomach doesn't know the difference.

• Separation anxiety *Don'ts*: Don't admonish, scold, berate, ridicule or try to use adult logic.

The kindest cut: tips for haircuts without tears. Many aspects of a hair salon or barber shop are similar to a doctor's or dentist's office: strange furniture, scary tools of the trade, unfamiliar chemical smells and potentially long, anxious waits. If getting gorgeous requires an afternoon of anguish, ask the stylist for these accommodations:

• Don't use the word "cut." Children know that cuts hurt. A cut finger hurts, a cut knee hurts; it follows that a haircut will hurt. Talk instead about getting her hair shortened, trimmed, tidied up, styled. She's getting her hair prettied up for the visit to Grandma's (or school or Thanksgiving) or lightened up for summer, or simply getting it out of her eyes.

• The typical salon chair that goes up and down and all around may not only be a vestibular problem—and his feet probably don't touch the footrest—but also resembles the chair at the dentist's office. Ask the stylist to offer a stationary stool or chair with a solid footrest at the child's height.

• The salon chair is likely much larger than he is. Downsize the seating area by tucking a pillow on either side of him and/or in his lap.

• Ask your stylist to stash away curling irons, scissors, hair dryers and other gear she will not be using for your child. Shiny metal implements may evoke doctor or dentist office associations. Skip the cape and the neck tape if the smell or texture seems to bother him.

• Ask that your child face away from the mirror during the haircut. Seeing sharp scissors or clippers flying about near his eyes and ears may be terrifying.

- Plastic-handled or covered-handle scissors and plastic, rather than metal combs, can reduce the amount of glare that can bounce off cutting/grooming utensils.

- Ask for an appointment at the slowest time of day and ask that overhead music be turned down or off. Ask for extra time to ensure the child does not feel rushed or forced.

- But don't schedule an appointment for a time when your child is likely to be tired (end of day or right before nap), hungry (right before lunch) or unhappy (is missing his favorite show).

- Call ahead to ensure that the stylist is running on time. Ask that everything be ready to go when you walk in so there is no anxiety-building wait.

- Offer a hand-held game or a board book as a distraction.

- Ask ahead of time if the salon offers treats or rewards afterward. If it's something your child is not allowed to have (sugar, allergy trigger, nonkosher), ask that it not be offered, or that a substitute item be offered (such as sticker).

- Take a fresh shirt to the salon with you. Those tiny leftovers hairs around the collar drive even NTs crazy.

- Between trims: Buy an inexpensive doll at a garage sale or thrift shop and let your child give the doll a haircut. If he doesn't handle scissors yet, he can still pantomime the haircut. Repeat the haircut simulations from time to time between actual haircuts.

Tips for reluctant shampooers. Even the happiest and most willing of bath babies may balk at shampoo time. This very invasive but necessary grooming routine can seem like a battlefield, but there are things you can do to ease the path towards her being able to tolerate it.

- Water coming toward the face area can feel aggressive. Offer earplugs, goggles, swim mask (covering his eyes not only keeps the water out but allows him to keep his eyes open if he's the type who fears surprises).

- Have your child lie down in the tub with just a few inches of water and wash from the back, bringing nothing into her field of vision.

- Let him wear his clothes, swimsuit, pajamas, whatever he chooses. The weight of the wet clothes may help proprioceptively. Or offer a wet towel or blanket.

- Use small amounts of shampoo to reduce rinse time.

- If rinsing with a cup, tell your child how many cupfuls you'll need to get her rinsed, then count. Knowing exactly when the torture is going to end may help her get through it.

- When rinsing with a cup, hold the cup lightly but directly to the scalp so the water is flowing but not striking the head. A measuring cup with a pour spout can help you better direct the flow of water.

- Commercial shampoos are heavily scented and even kid fragrances like bubble gum may be offensive. Many unscented, hypoallergenic shampoos are available via the Internet or at a local natural foods store.

- Don't insist on washing his hair with every bath or shower. Once or twice a week is sufficient for most children; knowing that the interval is infrequent may decrease resistance.

- Test the water temperature to ensure that it is not too cool or too hot (for her—not you). Warm the shampoo in your hands before applying; it may feel cold straight from the bottle, or the oozing sensation on her head may be disturbing.

- If the rubbing/massaging motion of shampooing bothers him, ask if he would rather do it himself.

- Try a car wash sponge for wetting and rinsing. Let her play with the sponge when you are done washing her hair.

- If you use a hand-held sprayer or squirt bottle, let him spray you back. It's just water, right? A little silliness goes a long way.

- Have everything you need ready before you start (small checklist may help: shampoo, towel, washcloth to hold over face, goggles or bath visor, etc.) If you are fumbling, it only adds to their anxiety.

- If your child tends to dump or ingest substances, remove shampoo from flip-top or screw-open bottles and place in a locking pump bottle. Keep out of sight between washings.

- Try out some of the "alternative" hair shampooing products. Dry-shampoo products that you spray on and brush out might work for those times when regular shampoo just doesn't happen. Or, try one of the no-rinse shampoo products available: apply shampoo, lather up and towel out. Find products such as these easily through Internet shopping outlets.

Nail trimming. As with the haircut, avoid using the word "cut." Explain that the nails need to be shortened, trimmed or tidied. Other ideas include:

- Always clip after bath or shower when nails are soft.

- If doing all ten fingers or toes at once is intolerable, do one a day in constant rotation as part of the general bedtime routine. Work up to two per day, etc.

- As early as possible, encourage the child to do it herself.

- Stabilizing the finger over the edge of a hard surface such as a counter, table, book or knee may help.

- Have Dad or a sibling trim their nails at the same time. They can take turns.

- Recite a rhyme, poem or story. Customize something like "This Little Piggy," "This Little Ninja" or "The Ants Go Marching" to suit him.

- Try it while they are totally engrossed in their favorite TV show.

- The fine-paper side of an emery board may be more tolerable and has the added benefit of eliminating sharp snags that may result from conventional clipping. Keep up with it on an every-few-days basis. Children's nails grow fast!

- When all else fails, do it while they are asleep.

- Search the Internet for adaptive devices. Comfort Care Baby Nail Clippers by The First Years come with an attached magnifying glass (decreases the chance of nipping tender skin) and large grippers for better control. LilNipper Clippers are plastic-encased clippers with a slot in the faceplate that the child slides his finger into, never actually seeing the clipping mechanism. Munchkin Safety Nail Clipper has a plastic safety guard and a safety-grip ring underneath to slip your finger through, steadying the clipper.

Just Take a Bite is the plaintive title of Lori Ernsperger's 2004 book, one to which many parents will instantly relate. Dr. Ernsperger, an autism and behavioral consultant, and co-author Tania Stegen-Hanson, a pediatric occupational therapist, offer answers to clashes over food aversions and eating challenges. They suggest some of the following tactics to try with your resistant eater:

- Develop a written mealtime schedule that includes snack times. The child can eat only during these times.
- Offer one preferred food at each meal/snack.
- Restrict milk and juice between meals.
- Parents and siblings eat together.
- Do not force the child to eat.
- Use measuring cups and spoons at each meal to ensure that the portion size is age appropriate.
- Involve the child with mealtime preparation.
- Remove the child if he or she is disrupting the meal.
- Provide the child with several opportunities during the day to learn about new foods. The education extends beyond eating to creating a food-rich environment.
- Ensure that the child's feet can touch the floor or footrest: Use an appropriately sized table and chairs that provide adequate proprioceptive stimulation.

Helpful eating adaptations. Poor oral-motor or fine motor control are contributing factors that can also make mealtimes difficult. Adaptive utensils can help.

- Websites like www.elderstore.net carry weighted utensils, as well as utensils with swivel heads, twisty handles and other accommodations. Also available: weighted cups, spout cups (a grown-up version of the "sippy cup"), double handled "thumbs-up" insulated cups.

- Homemade adaptations to help with grip might include poking the handle of the utensil through a foam or rubber ball, or covering the handle with some rubber tubing or pipe insulation foam.

- To keep her plate or bowl from slip-sliding away, place it on a foam-backed vinyl placemat, a wet washcloth or textured shelf liner paper.

- Or, attach no-slip devices to the bottom of a few special plates just for her: cork, bathtub appliqués or small suction cups are a few things to try.

- Decrease the distance from plate to mouth by placing the plate on a box, phone book, etc. Or raise the height of the table.

- Being seated in a straddle position across a bench or bolster may allow more upper body control. Because feet or knees must be firmly planted on the floor, this will work best at a child-sized table.

  Note: If you find yourself resisting this idea because it means that the family does not eat all together at the table, think a moment about separating issues and goals. Is the goal helping your child achieve independence in feeding himself or is the goal to have family together time at the table? Either is legitimate. But one is likely a temporary accommodation that can, with patience, lead to the other.

Food filosophy for finickies. Narrow food preferences: most kids with autism have them, and the usual tactics generally don't work with our kids. Ellen says she could offer her son a "broccoli forest" or a cheese sandwich with a raisin face 8,000 times and he would still be looking at it saying: "It's broccoli. Why are you playing with food?"

As with academic or other new areas, approaching the subject of eating or new foods through your child's area of interest may be worth a try. Here are a few ideas.

- Choose a flavor, taste or color that she does like and ask her to help you plan a whole meal around that flavor. Some examples:

  ~ All lemon menu: Fish, chicken or pasta with a lemon marinade or sauce, lemon-poppyseed muffins or quick bread, lemon pie or sorbet, lemonade

  ~ All orange menu: Salmon, yams, carrots, peaches and cantaloupe, pumpkin pie, orange sherbet, orange juice (yeah, we know, it's really yellow)

- Whether or not your child eats a single bite of her special meal is not important. Contributing to the food preparation process is, as is her broadening awareness of the vast variety of food possibilities available to her. For some kids, just being in the same room with the different foods may be success at first.

- Use a favorite food as an introduction to a wider variety of foods around it. If he just loves hamburgers:

  ~ Pick up menus from restaurants offering lots of burger choices. Talk about the different kinds of burgers offered—mushroom, cheese, gardenburger.

  ~ Ask friends or family members what kinds of condiments they like on their burgers and record the answers, maybe even make a graph.

  ~ Go on the Internet and find facts about burgers: Who invented the hamburger? Is there a Guiness record for hamburger eating? How many hamburgers are eaten in the United States each year? Where is the Hamburger Hall of Fame (yes, there is one)?

~ Plan a week of menus: Hamburgers are the main dish every night, but your child has to think up the side dishes. (He doesn't have to eat them—just think them up.) You can make suggestions to help him along—french fries, green salad, baked beans—but then let him take over. His responses may surprise you. And yes, you do need to cook whatever he suggests, however bizarre the combination may be to you.

• Spark interest in kitchen activities through recipes for nonfood items. They won't carry any *Will-I-be-asked-to-eat-it?* angst, so children often respond more quickly than with edible items. These might include: bubble solutions, facials, potpourri, doggie treats, play clay or dough, soap or bath salts.

You don't have to brush *all* your teeth, our dentist tells us—only the ones you want to keep. Oral defensiveness is a sensory difficulty that can make it hard for a child to tolerate foreign objects, or invasive tactile or gustatory (taste) sensations in his mouth. Tooth-brushing can be an ordeal for such children, but it is also essential to good health. To help a resistant brusher, try these tips:

• Remember that the purpose of brushing is to remove bacteria, and a toothbrush is just a tool for doing that. It's not the only tool, and there is no one "right" toothbrush. You can try:

~ Different shaped and angled toothbrushes

~ Different-shaped heads

~ Different consistency of bristles (most kids prefer soft)

~ No brush at all. Use a piece of gauze or washcloth wrapped around a finger. Dip it in toothpaste, flouride wash, or just plain water if that's all your child will tolerate. You'll still be removing a large amount of bacteria.

~ A battery-operated toothbrush. Many children find the vibration soothing, although some find it irritating.

~ Adaptive toothbrushes such as the Nuk toothbrush trainer (rubber latex brush) or Nuk massage brush, or the Collis-Curve™ Toothbrush, which brushes on all three sides at once (www.colliscurve.com). Another is the sixty-second TimeMachine Toothbrush, a timer toothbrush that brushes front, back and chewing surfaces of both upper and lower teeth at the same time. Available from Magical Toys and Products, www.magicaltoysandproducts.com, www.bestbabystore.com and other websites.

- Brush with warm water rather than cool to reduce sensitivity.

- Try different types and flavors of toothpaste. Paste may be too gritty but gel may be just right. And remember that proper brushing technique is much more important than whatever toothpaste you choose.

- If your child is sensitive to food dyes, artificial sweeteners and other substances, be aware that many common-brand toothpastes contain such ingredients. The FDA does not require toothpaste to be labeled as such, but if the paste has stripes, blue specklies or a pink glow, you can bet it contains dye.

- If brushing all the teeth at the same time is too overwhelming, break it up. Brush just the bottoms, take a two-minute break (or five or ten), then come back and brush the tops. Break down further as needed.

- Sing a short song with each section as a way of letting your child know how long it will take. Suggestions: "Bingo," "Farmer in the Dell," "Old McDonald," "Down by the Bay," "Five Little Ducks," or any one of numerous ditties adapted from "Row, Row, Row Your Boat" or "Twinkle Twinkle Little Star" (see the two that follow).

- Provide a visual chart illustrating each step of the tooth brushing process; helps build independence and self-esteem.

- Provide assistance and stability if needed. Stand behind rather than in front of your child to help, as the dentist does. Let him rest his head against you. Letting him sit may make it easier.

- Follow up tooth-brushing with a pleasant, anticipated activity (such as reading together or listening to music).

Teeth-brushing songs:
Sung to: "Row, Row, Row Your Boat"

Brush, Brush, Brush Your Teeth,

'til they're shiny bright.

They'll be healthy, they'll be strong,

If you treat them right.

Brush, brush brush your teeth.

Keep them clean each day.

Then you'll have a pretty smile,

And healthy teeth all day.

Brush, brush, brush your teeth,

After every meal.

The more you brush,

The more you floss (brush),

The better you will feel.

Brush, brush, brush your teeth,

After every meal.

Whiter, fresher, healthy teeth

Oh, how clean they feel.

Sung to: "Twinkle, Twinkle Little Star"

> Sparkle, sparkle, little teeth,
> Some above and some beneath.
> Brush them all at every meal,
> Clean and fresh they'll always feel.
>
> Sparkle, sparkle, little teeth,
> Some above and some beneath.
> Got my toothpaste, got my brush,
> I won't hurry, I won't rush.
>
> Making sure my teeth are clean,
> Front and back and in between.
> When I brush for quite a while,
> I will have a happy smile!

Button up, buckle up, make it snappy. Common clothing fasteners can be uncommonly challenging for children (of all ages!) with fine motor difficulties. Scratchy zippers and tags, cold snaps and bumpy buttons may be tactilely irritating as well. In her early years, it will not be the most important issue on her plate. An "if you can't beat 'em, join 'em" attitude is fine. It's more important that she gain the independence of being able to dress herself, so provide her with clothes that don't require fasteners: pull-on pants, T-shirts, skirts and dresses, cardigan jackets and sweaters that can be worn open. Then ease her into the world of fasteners.

- Provide a mirror so she can see what she is doing from an angle other than looking down.
- Start with Velcro® closures.
- Look for starter clothes with large zippers or buttons.

Tip: If you are handy with a sewing machine, you can enlarge the buttonholes on ready-made clothes and change out the buttons for larger ones.

- Focusing on the task may be easier from a sitting position, possibly with back stabilized against the wall or a chair.

- Start the process for her, i.e., thread the zipper, then let her pull it up. Attach a large zipper pull for better grip.

- Other clothing adaptations:

  ~ Tube socks, which don't require placing the heel.

  ~ Seamless socks for ultra-sensitive feet; can be found on websites for diabetic or orthopedic care (they are made for children who wear leg braces).

  ~ Open-ended sleeves, wide, no cuffs.

Managing the hospital visit. It's a fact of life: Kids will be kids and sometimes accidents happen that require a trip to the hospital or the emergency room. Before this situation happens with your child with ASD, prepare a handy one-page summary sheet you can provide to the hospital staff to quickly acquaint them to your child and how to best help your child through the experience. Keep a copy in the car at all times. Include:

- A general description of autism spectrum disorders.

- Your child's specific strengths and weaknesses.

- How your child processes instructions, e.g., visually rather than through auditory channels.

- Your child's need for extra time in processing verbal instructions.

- Sensory sensitivities: noise, shiny objects, the hum of testing equipment, how touch affects him and which kind is best (e.g., light or more firm), taste, smell or texture, etc.

- Your child's literal interpretation of expressions (e.g., "Jump right up here").

- Your child's lack of eye contact and difficulty understanding social cues.

- Any stims or echolalia, especially in stressful situations.
- Distress over changes in routine.
- Motor skills challenges.
- Signs of a meltdown and how to handle one if it occurs, including use of restraints.

Hospital visits may never be easy for a child with autism, but with a little planning, you can make it go more smoothly for everyone involved.

Help for a runny nose. Some kids seem to have a perpetually runny nose throughout the winter, and difficulty with hygiene only opens the door to ridicule from classmates. The child may not even be aware of the mess, and if he is, may have trouble using water for facial cleanup. Provide the child with a box of hypoallergenic wipes so he can clean up independently, and have a mirror in the classroom or at home to help him see what needs to be done.

Let's get this potty started! Toilet training is a frequent topic of conversation among parents of young children during their toddler years. For your child with ASD, sensory, motor and perceptual differences make this a developmental milestone filled with challenges.

Many ideas associated with toilet training are listed below. Beforehand, though, we want to impress upon you two thoughts:

1. As much as you would like this to happen on some sort of socially accepted timetable, the plain truth of the matter is that kids will become toilet trained when *they* are ready. Wait until a child is at least eighteen months old before even thinking of potty training. Once started, if all of your very creative and very appropriate efforts are not working, consider that you may be trying too hard, too early. Give it a rest and try again in another couple of months.

2. That said, keep in mind that a child who, at the age of four, five or seven is not yet toilet trained will be the

subject of peer ridicule that will grossly erode his or her self-esteem. Make toilet training a priority after age four and get help from a professional if you need it.

Signs that your child is ready to begin a toilet-training program.

- The child stays dry for longer periods of time.
- He seems to perceive a relationship between consuming fluids and when urination occurs.
- She shows visible signs of urinating or having a bowel movement (e.g., squatting, pulling at her pants, touching herself or crossing her legs).
- He shows interest or you see a difference in behavior in response to him seeing other people involved in toileting activities.
- The ability to sit for about five minutes during an activity.
- He can pull his pants up and down with assistance.
- She understands simple directions (e.g., "sit down" or "stand up").

The potty-training process. Before you start potty training, chart your child's urination patterns over a ten- to fourteen-day time period. This will help determine how long your child is staying dry, and also when urination is most likely to occur. You must be able to arrange a fair amount of time with your child to do nothing else but potty training. It is helpful to have two or even three people available to help.

Give your child plenty of liquids. This will encourage urination and will increase the opportunities to reward successful attempts. Place him on the potty at the first waking moment of the day, for about three to five minutes. Make this a fun time. Read stories, blow bubbles or play games. Use your data chart to gauge how frequently to put him back on the potty. If he is staying dry between sittings on the potty, expand the time gradually by a set increment of minutes.

If there is an accident, lessen the time between potty sittings to the previous amount of free time where he remained successful. After a few hours, if successful, you may want to put training pants on your child. Remember that potty training is a big step for a child. They have been peeing in those diapers for a long time. Habits don't die easily; be patient and be consistent.

A long list of related toilet training ideas follow; some alert you to the sensory issues involved with potty training a child with ASD. Others speak to encouragement, praise and reward. Hang in there!

1. Try to get your child to sit on the toilet with the lid down while he is still wearing diapers; then move on to sitting with the lid up and undressed.

2. Teach pre-toileting dressing skills first; many involve motor planning skills that need to be in place to manage the dressing/undressing sequence and fastening pants.

3. Don't potty train when there has been a major event; for example, Mom is back at work, you moved to a new house, or the child moved to a bigger bed. Likewise, if your child gets sick during training, all bets are off. Delay the routine and start again once he's well or changes are back to a minimum.

4. Choose a method and stick with it. Give any method at least several weeks to see if it works. However, if you don't see positive gains in two weeks, take a good look at your program for inconsistencies or errors and adjust accordingly.

5. Use underpants; they get wet and provide feedback to the child. To help protect the furniture, and maintain good hygiene, try plastic pants worn over the underwear, or plastic padding on the furniture while training takes place.

6. Consider how you dress the child during potty training. Potty training is easier in the summer because children have less clothing to deal with. Elastic-waist pants are a better clothing choice than those that may cause him to

have accidents while fumbling with zippers. He needs to be successful when he does the right thing.

7. Be a model. Children learn from example. If it is comfortable for you, provide your child with opportunities to see how the potty is effectively used. Or use siblings to model the correct behaviors for your child.

8. Use a positive approach and stay upbeat and supportive at all times. When you see appropriate behaviors, comment on them and reinforce them with specific verbal praise.

9. Use simple, concrete directives and be consistent with your language.

10. Expect some accidents and when they happen, remain calm. Never punish accidents; they're part of eventually getting it right. However, teach your child responsibility for his actions by having him help clean up a mess he created. Clean up with minimal social interaction. As strange as it may sound, the verbal attention can be reinforcing for some children.

11. Schedule a relaxing or low-stimulation activity just before scheduled toilet times so your child is more relaxed before starting the toilet training routine.

12. Teach using the toilet as an entire routine involving preparation and activities needed for completion, rather than just sitting on the toilet. Break the toilet-training program into parts your child can handle. For instance, going to bathroom and closing the door, undressing, toileting, dressing, washing hands, exiting the bathroom. Using a visual schedule will help promote independence. Cover your strip of visual cues with plastic, so they don't get wet, if you're posting them near the sink.

13. Avoid asking if the child needs to use the bathroom when the schedule indicates a toileting time. Until the child is trained, handing him a visual cue means that the potty routine starts.

14. Make sure the bathroom is seen as a relaxing place, and not loaded with tension. Check for any stressors that might influence your child (Bathroom fan? Glaring lights? Texture of the bathroom seat or carpeting/tile? Smells?)

15. If your child reacts negatively to sitting on the toilet, it may be in response to the feel of the seat, feeling unstable while on the toilet, being afraid of the noise from flushing or being afraid of falling into or touching the water.

    a. Use a stool so their feet are flat on a surface, at right angles to the floor, which supports their back.

    b. Change out the seat for a vinyl, padded one; consider a slightly smaller sized seat that is commonly available.

16. If your child impulsively jumps off the toilet to look at other things in the bathroom, place a small, plastic table over his lap once he sits down. Then give him a few favored toys or activities to play with on the table.

17. Be careful using perfumed soaps, lotions and wet wipes when completing the toileting routine. Some children are cued by the smell to engage in the related behavior. Smelling the perfume on their hands may prompt them to eliminate once outside the bathroom.

18. Eliminating in the toilet is one of the few tasks that you do NOT want the anxious child to focus on. Give her something else to focus attention on, such as a book or a toy. The more she thinks about eliminating, the more difficult it will be.

19. Think twice about using food as a reinforcer, as it may not be that enticing after a meal.

20. For children who eliminate several times per hour, because of a constant intake or food of liquids, consider incorporating scheduled intake of food and drink during the potty training program.

21. If you decide to use books or toys or a particular music CD to induce relaxation during the toileting routine,

make sure these items are not available to the child at any other time of the day.

22. If your child is too fascinated by flushing the toilet, make sure your picture cue shows not only when to flush, but how many times.

23. Handwashing: Use precise directions such as "use one squirt of soap" or "wash for one minute" (use a timer) if you find your child becomes stuck during this part of the sequence or uses it for play.

24. Is your child using too much toilet paper? Teach her to count out a specific number of sheets, or place a mark along the wall, several inches below the roll, then teach her to unroll the paper until the end touches the mark, then tear it off.

25. Once your child has learned to use the toilet properly, don't remove all the visual cues. Change the appearance to simpler visual prompts, or those that are more natural looking.

26. Avoid trying to toilet train a child at night when frequent or regular wetting in the daytime is still a problem. First things first.

27. Communicate any information to your child's teacher that may impact his toilet training program: unusual foods ingested, or new medications.

28. All caregivers, including grandmas, should consistently use the same toilet training methods. Teach them what you are doing and enlist their help and cooperation to maintain a consistent program.

Green magic. For little boys who are reluctant to use the toilet, try adding blue food coloring to the water in the bowl. When they pee it will turn green right before their eyes. Magic! For variety: red food coloring + pee = orange.

Muffle it. Keep a pair of earmuffs next to the toilet for reluctant trainees who can't tolerate the sound of the flushing.

Desperation is the mother of invention. A mom we know was becoming frantic because her son would not give in to bowel movements. It was becoming a serious health problem. The boy was quite bright and had a fascination with numbers. One desperate day, when the boy had managed a bowel movement in the toilet, Mom said, "Oh, look! It's in the shape of a 7!" That was all it took—end of problem.

Poop or get off the pot. Success! Your child is staying dry during the day, and perhaps even at night. You're ready to tackle problem #2. Here are some possible pitfalls to avoid:

- Be aware that for some children, the added pressure and weight of a diaper filled with waste can be calming and therefore, they will resist having a BM in the toilet.

- If your child has a BM in his pants within twenty minutes of exiting the bathroom, make the toilet training experience more relaxing. Longer time on the toilet will not help.

- Be careful with picture cues of waste in a toilet. Some individuals with autism may interpret this as meaning they can have a bowel movement anywhere, as long as they then dispose of the waste in the toilet. Use a picture cue that shows waste being expelled while sitting on the commode.

- If constipation is a problem, add more fruits, vegetables, whole grains and legumes to their diet, or try a natural bulk laxative, which is very gentle.

- Some children have real fears about BMs; they think their insides are coming out, or that they are losing parts of themselves. If this is the case, go slow. Try explaining the digestive system to the child, using visuals of the human body. A very popular book with lots of moms and kids is *Everyone Poops* by Taro Gomi.

- How much wiping is enough? As a rule of thumb, teach him to wipe three times. This may not be enough at first and the adult present can continue to clean up, if necessary. But as he becomes more adept, three times should be enough.

Staying dry at night. Teaching your child to stay dry at night involves some preplanning and a few minor routine changes as nighttime approaches. Keep in mind the following ideas as your put together a nighttime potty-training schedule for your child.

- Restrict liquids, including water, after 6 pm. If he's thirsty, give him only a few small sips.

- Schedule a toilet time immediately before he climbs into bed. Make it part of his bedtime routine, not an option.

- Once he's asleep, check him periodically to determine when he's urinating during the night; you'll probably see a pattern. Then wake him up consistently ten to fifteen minutes before that time and take him to the toilet to urinate. Do this without a lot of fuss.

- Incorporate a visual prompt into his nighttime toileting routine. Post it at eye level on the bathroom door and direct his attention to it every time he uses the toilet—day or night. Hand him a matching picture when you waken him during the night. This will build the foundation for eventually using visual cues to prompt independent toileting at night without adult intervention.

- Make sure the visual prompt is located where he can see it when he awakens during the night, reminding him to get up and use the toilet.

- Be sure to also teach him to respond to a picture that symbolizes "sleep" and post this so he can readily see it when he finishes his nighttime toilet visit. You want to make sure he returns to bed and goes back to sleep.

Using public restrooms. As if potty training wasn't tricky enough! Once you do establish a routine at home, you face the fresh challenge of making it work in a public setting. Facilities designers don't really set out to purposely make your life difficult, but it can seem that way, can't it? Sinks, toilets, soap and towel dispensers are too high or too far away to reach, automatic flushers and hand dryers shriek and scream at unpredictable intervals, the bathroom itself is cold, clammy and smelly, or overheated, fetid and smelly. Diapers starting to sound good again? Don't retreat; you can outwit the most thoughtless architect. Read on:

- Many public restrooms are now equipped with automatic-flush toilets. They operate by using an electronic eye to detect when the user has moved away from the toilet. Such toilets can be terrifying for children, especially if they are too small to prevent the electronic eye from tripping and the toilet flushes while they are on it. To prevent this, simply cover the electronic eye while your child uses the toilet. If you are not accompanying your child into the stall, carry a suction cup that fits over the eye, and show your child how to attach it. Practice at home.

- The Potty Poncho™ is a portable toilet seat protector with a rubberized vinyl backing that resists slipping on the toilet seat. It can be cleaned after each use with an anti-bacterial wipe or machine washed. It folds to fit into a small carrying case designed for the product. Start your child on it at home and then transition to public bathrooms. Has the added benefit of preventing your child's bottom from coming in contact with the toilet seat. www.pottyponcho.com

- Carry extra wipes for hand-washing (individually packaged towelettes or a travel package of baby wipes). Very few public restrooms are kid-accessible. The sinks are too high, the soap dispensers (when there is actually any soap in them) are mounted on the back wall; some sinks have faucets while some are motion detectors, paper towels dispensers can have confusing cranks or knobs that may or may not work. (Anyone out there listening? How about some simple step stools?) If your child is noise-sensitive, beware of electric hand dryers. Show them to your child immediately upon entering the restroom so she will not be spooked by the unexpected howling sound of someone using one while she is still in the stall. If necessary, put your hands over her ears.

- If your child is gravitationally insecure (doesn't like her feet off the ground), a public toilet where feet must dangle in mid-air may be an insurmountable challenge. Carrying a step stool around isn't practical. Go into the stall with your child, kneel on one knee and let her use your raised leg for a footrest.

• If your child is confused by restrooms that have multiple stalls (as in schools and public buildings) teach him or her to access the first open stall door.

• Knowing where the restroom is before you need it will ease your child's anxiety about "accidents." Upon reaching your destination, locate the nearest restroom and point it out to your child.

• Take "practice trips" to destinations you know to have kid-friendly facilities such as family bathrooms, private handicapped or single-user restrooms. Your child may feel more secure in a single locking room (more like home) than in a partitioned stall in an echoey-tiled room with a dozen other stalls.

> ~ Dads out in public with daughters face the most challenges. Think the situation out before you leave home.

Shopper on board. Grocery shopping can be a stressful activity for both moms and kids with autism. All the smells, shopping cart wheels squeaking or bumping, temperature changes. It can be a sensory minefield. Plus, kids often are just plain bored. One solution: let them help shop.

Take digital photos of the front panel of single grocery items, or simply cut out the labels from the box and glue them to index cards. Print the name of the item under the picture or photo to reinforce reading. Arrange the cards in the order of the aisles in the grocery store and let your child help find the needed items as you walk through the aisles. Keep the photos or cards in a box or pouch, and remember to devise a place for cards for those items 'found'. As skills increase, kids can independently find some items and return them to the cart. Or move from pictures and words to words only as comprehension increases.

Snappy comeback. No matter how carefully you manage your child's daily routine and activities, there will inevitably come the moment when he melts down in front of the disapproving eyes of your mother-in-law, neighbor or strangers in public. While we'd love to think that you have a hide of steel and are able to ignore the misplaced judgment of people who have never walked a meter in your shoes (let alone a mile), we also know that you may feel compelled to say something in your own defense. If so, having an arsenal of comebacks means you will never be left fumbling for words during those difficult moments.

While profanity may appeal, humor is better. We also favor the remark that reminds the listener that your child is not the first or last to lose his cool in such a manner. Some suggestions:

"Yep, it's the Theatrical Threes (Ferocious Fours), all right."

"She's really having a Monday, isn't she?"

"There he is, the next Richard Burton."

Remarks like these let the onlooker know that you have the situation in hand—without any help from them, thank you.

Some parents who prefer the silent treatment or are uncomfortable making verbal comments (too tempting?), yet still want to impart a measure of social awareness on ASD, calmly give out an "Autism Awareness" card that briefly explains that their child has autism, what it is and the behavioral manifestations of the disorder. These cards are available through a number of chapters of the Autism Society of America, www.autism-society.org.

When Mom or Dad is away. Mom or Dad being away on work- or family-related business travel can severely disrupt your routine-dependent child, enormously impacting the rest of his world. Here are a few ways to help him through it:

- Respect his anxieties and don't spring the trip on him as a surprise. Show him pictures of where you are going to be. If he has a favorite story character, role-play a parental business trip. What might Arthur think or do when his parent is away?

• Leave tape recordings (or videos) of yourself as touchstones. Read several of his favorite stories. Record a tape for each morning (or evening): "Good morning, Parker! It's Tuesday and today is the day you go to the library. Remember to return your book. Thanks for feeding Rover last night. Good job!"

• Set up prearranged times that you will call home, and then *do it at that time.* A nebulous "I'll call sometime" may create never-ending anxiety. Choose a time you know you can stick to, taking into account any time differences and your child's state of mind at different times of day. If hearing your voice right before bedtime sets off the waterworks, call right after breakfast, after school or after dinner.

• If Mom is going away and Dad will be the caregiver, ensure that he is apprised of the details of the child's daily schedule. (A visual chart is good for dads too!) Keep everything as familiar as possible, e.g., this is not the time to try new foods.

• If he has a familiar or favorite food that only you know how to make, make ahead and freeze so he can still have it while you are gone.

• Let your child know that while he is out of sight, he is certainly not out of mind. Leave small notes around the house in unexpected places that he will find over the course of your time away—under his pillow, in his sock drawer, in the cookie jar, folded into his towel. Keep the notes simple: "thinking of you," "you make me proud," "have a great day."

• Make your child a special photo item of yourself that is used only when you are away. If you have a computer that handles photographs, use iron-on transfer paper and a photo of yourself to create a pillowcase or sleep shirt she can use while you are gone.

• Take along a disposable camera and ask a colleague to take a few pictures of you in the course of your trip. Take photos of your hotel, the room, the view from the window or balcony, the bathroom. Include the airport or taxi. Use photos to put together a picture book for the next trip.

- If your child likes miniatures, bring him the items from your hotel room such as tiny bottles of shampoo, bars of soap, little bottles of ketchup or small jars of jam from room service. Cocktail napkins, tiny straws or swizzle sticks from the bar may also fascinate.

- Don't overlook unusual items like the shoe-polishing cloth, shower cap or barf bag from the airplane.

- Is your child a "collector?" If you travel more than occasionally, you can encourage an interest in new places by bringing him a small souvenir from each place—spoons, thimbles, snow globes and "greetings from" postcards are common, inexpensive items found virtually everywhere.

- Your being away is not only hard on your child but may be hard on the substitute caregiver as well. Don't extend your trip unnecessarily.

- Let your child know exactly when your absence will end. X'ing off the days on a calendar is one way. Or, relate it to his daily routine by telling him, "Mom will be back after three sleeps." (If naps are still part of the routine, be sure to specify "night sleeps.")

Dress rehearsal. A full-blown dress rehearsal at home for important events such as weddings, parties or formal dinners is worth the effort. An hour before Cousin Emma walks down the aisle is not a good time to find out that your son's suit pants ride up his bottom when he sits, the clip-on tie bothers his throat, the dress socks are too tight and the shirt cuffs are too short. (*Tips:* "Real" ties that slip under the collar will lie smoothly and allow the top button of the shirt to be left open, short-sleeved shirts are fine for your child and so are any kind of socks that keep him comfortable— who's going to be looking at his feet anyway?) Other helpful ideas:

- First, be honest about whether your child is ready to attend such an event. If he truly can't keep all four legs of his chair on the floor, gets easily overloaded in a room full of people and noise, still thinks a fork is for combing hair and eats applesauce with his fingers, it may be kinder to all involved to call in the sitter.

- Visit the venue—restaurant, house of worship—beforehand to give her a visual image.

- Explain what will happen at the event, whether wedding, bar mitzvah, grandparent's birthday, or family reunion. What will she be expected to do? Sit quietly during the service, sign a guest book, get food from a buffet?

- If possible, arrange seating where she will be able to see the event. However, if you think she may not make it through the entire event, sit where she can be taken out unobtrusively.

- Preview the menu and if it is not appropriate for your child, ask the hotel or restaurant for a special meal. Most are glad to do it. Offer to pay separately. If special arrangements are not possible, bring something for your child as inconspicuously as possible or feed her beforehand so she is not sitting around ravenously watching everyone else eat. When you've done what you can, don't sweat it further. Holidays and events are so exciting for many children that they don't eat much anyway.

- Teach him a simple introduction and, if he can tolerate it, a handshake.

- Let him know there will be a lot of people there, but he doesn't have to hug or kiss anyone if he doesn't want to, especially strangers. Then stay close to support him in this. "Josh prefers not to hug," delivered in a pleasant, unapologetic tone of voice is perfectly acceptable.

- Give appropriate fifteen-, ten- and five-minute warnings, then leave while he's still having fun and the memories will be good. In other words, before the "too-much-party" meltdown.

- Having him tell the host "thank you for inviting me" before leaving puts nice closure on the event.

Never forget that autism has given your child the gifts of rote memory, imitative speech and literal interpretation. Refrain from wondering aloud in the car on the way to the party if Uncle Joe will over-imbibe as usual, unless you want to hear little Hannah check in later with "I want to sit with Uncle Joe so I can see if he really does drink like a fish!"

We are fam-i-ly. Inevitably, there will be times when it seems to your neuro-typical child that his sibling with autism receives a disproportional amount of Mom's attention. Quell sibling rivalry and resentment by ensuring that they have a shared history of good times to fall back on during the stormy times.

Planning shared activities that are fun for both of them can seem challenging when their ages and abilities may be vastly different. The author's two sons are almost five years apart in age (the younger son is the one with autism), and although many family outings were "divide and conquer," the boys had no trouble coming up with a long list of fun stuff they do together. Here are some of their suggestions:

- Visiting local rock-clad river beaches and skipping stones, throwing rocks in the river, or using their sling shots
- Visiting amusement parks with carnival rides and game arcades
- Doing jigsaw puzzles
- Making forts out of large appliance boxes
- Older brother was pitcher/assistant coach for younger brother's baseball team
- Local farm experiences: picking blueberries and apples, although sometimes throwing and splatting the rotten apples on the tree trunks was more fun than picking, and sometimes sticking their heads in the sprinklers was a better time than picking
- Cooking a spaghetti dinner or baking brownies

- Sleeping over in each other's rooms or at Grandma's
- Making a film with the camcorder

Reinforce all the good memories with a small photo album they can keep in their nightstand. Update as needed.

Equal time. Siblings are important members of the family team, frequently offering remarkable support and advocacy for their brother or sister with autism. But they are also children with needs and uncertainties. Set aside "dates" for them—regularly scheduled special times when they get your undivided attention to do something of their choosing. It could be dinner out on Wednesdays, a bike ride on Saturday mornings, a once- or twice-a-month movie or browsing the used bookstore. Being secure in their individual importance to you helps them weather the difficult times with their sibling and strengthens their motivation to advocate.

The newspaper: window on the world. It is undeniable that much of what appears in the newspaper is disturbing to children, above their reading comprehension level or simply not of interest. But there is still much that is relevant to a child. The process of acclimating your child to the newspaper may be a long one, so start 'em young and take it slowly.

- Comics and cartoons for children come to mind first. Their visual orientation will naturally draw some children with autism. Choose a child-oriented strip and follow it every day or every Sunday. After a while, you can follow up with a suggestion that your child draw his own cartoon or comic strip.

- Look for kid-appropriate photos to discuss. What do you think is happening here? Oh, look—it's the park near our house! And here is an interesting flower show going on; shall we visit it? This baseball player has your favorite number on his jersey. What do you think this policeman is trying to do?

- The weather report is always relevant and is pictorially represented in many papers. Have your child try to predict from the pictures whether it is going to be sunny, cloudy, rainy, hot or cold. How hot/cold was it yesterday/last night? What will the weather be in Grandma's city? Why is the temperature eighty-five degrees in Australia when it is twenty degrees here?

- Articles or weekly columns about pet care, kid-friendly websites or new children's books by a favorite author may be of interest.

- Read movie reviews of the latest family-appropriate movies, plus any "making-of" features or stories about the actors in a favorite film.

- Scan the sports section for stories about kids. Or, follow a favorite team, checking their stats each day.

  ~ If your child does show an interest in a sports team, take the opportunity to point out how sports phraseology (idioms) find their way into our everyday language. For instance: When someone says they are "way off-base," they mean they are wrong about something. If someone makes a "ballpark estimate," it means they're making a guess.

To hug or not to hug. All children nowadays are taught, under the banner of "stranger danger" and child abuse prevention, to protest any kind of touch that makes them uncomfortable. Children with autism experience this tenfold. Many have an aversion to being hugged and kissed, even when it is by well-meaning relatives or teachers whom they may or may not know very well. The reasons may be many: the contact came without warning, the person doing the hugging smells funny, the touch is too light or too harsh, it disturbs his vestibular or proprioceptive equilibrium.

- Inform and enforce. Let family members and those in daily contact with him know that hugging and other touching must be at his discretion only. Be prepared to be firm with Aunt Rose who insists it's "dust a wittle hug-hug!!"

- Always give him the choice, then validate that choice. Ask, "Is it okay if I give you a hug?" If the answer is no, respond with a pleasant, "That's okay!" (Because it is.) If he does agree to the hug, a simple "thank you" is appropriate.

- Give a warning before touching: "I'm going to boost you up to the car seat now, okay?"

- Use firm pressure when touching. In this regard, sometimes Dad will have more luck with getting cooperation than Mom, whose touch may be lighter. Many children prefer Dad's help in the bathtub or swimming pool for just this reason.

> Davis loved his grandma and was willing to accept hugs, but at first it was only if he "backed into it." That is, instead of the usual chest-to-chest hug, he backed into the embrace. Grandma accepted this as completely normal and wonderful, and in time he was able to transition to typical hugging.

Birthday thoughts and strategies. The contemporary culture of holding birthday parties outside the home is one that may be out of the question for your ASD child. Arcades, play zones, movie theatres and bowling alleys are inherently crowded and may be unendurably noisy. Partying at home allows you to control all the factors that influence your child's behavior, which goes a long way toward ensuring a happy and memorable occasion that will be just right for him. It won't involve any more cost than a go-somewhere party and it needn't involve grotesque effort, either.

The activity.

Keep the party at your child's developmental, not chronological age. He may be more comfortable with parallel rather than interactive play, open-ended rather than structured play, fun stuff that doesn't require a lot of language. If so, forego competitive games with rules and scorekeeping. Opt for active, sensory-filled activities such as a bounce house (rent from a party company), bubble machine (chase 'em! poke 'em! tackle 'em!), sand table or box, water gun fight and/or slip 'n' slide, homemade ball pit (inflatable pool filled with plastic balls), tug-o-war. If you have a large wall, cover it with butcher paper and provide crayons and markers for the guests to make the biggest-ever birthday card. Or, cover a table with plain fabric and have guests doodle and sign the tablecloth with fabric pens or paints (handprints are always fun).

Make traditional party elements active rather than passive.

- Cupcakes have advantages over the traditional frosting-encased cake. They are just the right portion size for kids, and decorating them is a party activity in itself most kids just love. Cupcakes freeze well, so you can make them ahead of time and thaw on the day of the party. Provide small bowls of frosting, sprinkles, chopped nuts or candies as ppropriate. And of course a candle for the birthday child. Would he or she enjoy those trick candles that keep relighting themselves? Talk about prolonging the moment! Available at party stores. *See Footnote below on birthday cakes.*

- The forgettable junk in those ubiquitous "goody bags" may hold a child's interest in the short term, but doesn't it more often end up in a raucous tussle with your vacuum cleaner? Rather than merely handing guests a trinket or two on the way out, make 'em work for their loot. Consider two alternatives: the pinata and the treasure chest. Making a piñata or plotting the hunt are enjoyable lead-up events that involve your child in the big picture of party planning.

  ~ Make your own piñata from a grocery bag with handles, involving your child at any level at which he is able to participate. You don't have to be an artist and it doesn't take long. For instance, an octopus face with crepe paper tentacles couldn't be simpler. Or use clip art enlarged on the copier a couple of times. Or spray paint the bag and add stickers. Whether the artwork is pristine—or even recognizable—is not important. It's going to get smashed in a matter of minutes, right?

  ~ A treasure hunt has similar allure. Siblings or other family members can get involved by creating the clues and setting up the hunt. Clues should be at the birthday child's level of representation: photos, drawings, single words, simple rhymes. Any sturdy container will do for the chest; go Rubbermaid or shop Goodwill for a suitably battered box or trunk.

The guest list.

You know best how much commotion your child can handle; if a small celebration is what he needs be ruthless about limiting the guest list to an appropriate number (the old rule is age +1). Be clear on the invitation that you are including the guest and one parent only. And be considerate—if you aren't inviting his whole class, mail the invitations; do not send them to school.

The party's o-o-over.

Again, you know best how much commotion your child can handle. Put a clear end time on the invitation and, if parents are dropping their child off, remind them. Have a quiet closing activity (sorting or swapping toys and candy from the pinata) before cheerily announcing "That's all, folks!" If parents accompanying children linger past the end time, it's okay to make a point of telling every-one "thanks so much for coming; Drew was such a fun guest; Kyra can't wait to read the Arthur book," and begin cleaning up.

The gifting.

Some guests will inquire as to what the birthday child likes. Do not be bashful about steering them towards your child's interests, which may be limited. There's nothing to be gained by being coy; gifts that have no meaning for him may confuse and upset him, and if he likes airplanes or she likes hats, getting six of them will be sheer delight. At the same time, be prepared to handle his or her reaction to a gift that may have no meaning.

- Giving your party a theme is an easy way of suggesting gifts that will appeal. A theme can be as simple as having the invitations, paper plates and napkins, pinata/treasure hunt carry a common motif: pirates, horses, fire trucks, flowers, dinosaurs, etc.

• At a minimum, your child needs to be able to say "thank you" to each guest for the gift. It may be difficult for her to understand why she must acknowledge a gift she doesn't like. It's never too early to start telling her that part of the gift is the effort the guest went to in trying to choose something thoughtful. Rehearsing the scenario beforehand may help. Round up items from around the house and role play opening a variety of gifts.

Ending on the right note.

In addition to saying thank you for the gift, saying "thank you for coming" puts an end bracket on the event for both the guest and the host.

Footnote: And speaking of cake. It may be traditional but whose party is it anyway? If your little one is indifferent to cake, substitute something else. Anything edible accompanied by "Happy Birthday" and a candle to blow out is dandy. Over the years, we've seen birthday pie, birthday watermelon, birthday cookies, brownies, ice cream sundaes, popsicles, and Three Musketeers bars. Now really, what could be sillier than worrying about whether guests will be "disappointed" if they don't get cake?

Consider also that your child's idea of fun with a cake might involve something other than eating it. In their younger years, the author's two sons had other ideas. Son #1 wanted to eat his cake without benefit of fork or hands—in other words, face first into the frosting. Yes, it was allowed—once, and at a family-only celebration, not a party. The photos were priceless. Son #2 disliked cake but loved construction equipment. He wanted a thickly frosted cake with a construction motif, so he could plow the frosting and excavate the cake using Hot Wheels vehicles as cake toppers. Rock candy embellishments added to the realism. The video was priceless. Always let the good times roll and everyone will have a better time—including you!

Uncommon gifts for uncommon kids. Birthdays and holidays can be gift-giving challenges if you have a child with ASD whose interests don't fall neatly into the typical toy store catalog. Think outside the traditional gift-box and in the direction of your child's real interests; ordinary items unusually presented can inspire true glee. The following ideas were hits within Ellen's family and might appeal to your child too.

- Everyday items that reinforce sensory experiences make for intriguing gifts, and almost anything in a surprisingly generous quantity is fun. For instance, our son's most beloved gift for several years running was a basket of many cans of shaving cream, to dispense in any quantity desired in bathtub, driveway, or kitchen sink. Other comers in this category were balloons (blow up a hundred and he gets to pop them all at once) and marshmallows (he never actually ate one; his shtick was melting them in the campfire. Incinerating an entire package without hearing "you're wasting them!" delighted him.).

- Flashlights are cool, another ordinary sensory item that can become extraordinary. Can you ever actually find one when you need it? Give a whole basket full of flashlights. Even modern kids can succumb to the simple diversion of lights-off flashlight tag, and "light shows" on the ceilings and walls, with or without music. Enhance the experience with a book like Frank Jacobs' *Fun with Hand Shadows* or Bill Mayer's *Shadow Games*.

- Pirate Treasure. The year my costume jewelry kept disappearing was the year I discovered that my kids were borrowing it for pirate booty. I got my stuff back via a garage sale, which provided me with an old treasure chest-style jewelry box and the loot to fill it. Old thrift store jewelry is perfect too, or just ask each of your friends for one piece they never wear. Or fill the chest with whatever else your child enjoys most. Then go all the way—bury or hide the chest. Devise a treasure map or series of clues the child/children must decode to get to the loot. The process is a gift in itself. If your child/children are young or nonreaders, the clues can be photographs or drawings. As they learn to read and become more proficient, the clues increase in complexity.

- The most ordinary item in an unexpected container can spark amusement. Try a toolbox filled with homemade cookies, a six-pack cooler filled with socks; a hollowed out pumpkin with—what else?—a Cinderella doll inside; or a child's rain boot, lined with tissue and filled with candy and a fistful of character or favorite-color toothbrushes (which she gets to open all at the same time if she wants to).

Remember too that an equally important piece of the gifting process is the giving part. The child with autism already struggles to understand and interpret the feelings of others. "What do you think Dad would like?" may be a question whose answer is simply beyond their reach. But it is not a reason to leave them out of the gifting process "for now." "Later" may not come without long, loving and gentle repetition and reinforcement. Start now by having them participate in the creation of gifts that are guaranteed to please. Seeing expressions of pleasure and receiving profuse thanks directed specifically at them will eventually imprint.

> *Note:* Guaranteed-pleaser gifts are those that contain a piece of the giver, such as a photo snow globe. Kids can help select the photos and cut them to shape. The globes are usually double-sided, so the child can decide what goes on each side. Maybe one side is a current photo and the other side is a baby photo. Maybe one side is a miniature piece of their artwork or thumbprint heart. *Variations:* photo bobbleheads, photo or artwork Christmas tree ornaments, calendars or lockets.

You are mighty special. Any efforts we, as parents and teachers, take to enhance a child's self-esteem are simply invaluable. Take that artwork off the refrigerator or out of the pile in the corner of the classroom: Having the child's work professionally framed says, "You are mighty special." Plus, the constant stream of visitors' attention—especially at home—validates their efforts over and over.

Safe in the yard. Set up visual boundaries defining the area in which your child may safely play.

- Walk around the perimeter of the safe play area with your child; do it every day or every few days until it is imprinted.

- Paint or make a large red STOP sign at the end of the driveway.

- Use a line of orange traffic or sports cones to define boundaries.

- Spray-paint a bright orange or yellow line around the boundaries of the yard. If on the lawn, yes, it will have to be reapplied every couple of mowings.

Home safety for escape artists and acrobats. If your home feels like an obstacle course in the face of your perpetual-motion, master-of-disaster child, heed these safety suggestions from parents like you:

- Replace plate glass windows with unbreakable glass, plexiglass or glass blocks.

- Cover holes in the wall with laminated artwork bolted to the wall with moulding.

- Bolt your entertainment center to the wall and install a plexiglass door on it to prevent breakage or damage to television, stereo, etc.

- Install TOT LOCKS on cabinets. They install on the inside of the cabinet and are invisible on the outside. They are opened by using a magnetic device.

- Yes, there is kid-proof fencing. One family's story: "We have a fence in our front yard so my daughter cannot escape. It is made of PVC material. She squeezed through that by bending the material, so we put metal rods down inside them. The locks (there are three) to the gate are on the outside. Now she is safe."

- Keep your little Houdini safely strapped into the car with a "bus vest," which zips in the back and is then hooked into

the seat belt system. See this and other related items at
http://www.ezonpro.com/products/schoolBus/vestClosure.shtml.

- Thwart furniture-flippers with built-in beds, built-in
  shelving and built-in storage. Sink the bed and enclose the
  corners to further prevent mattress removal.

When your child isn't sleeping. Anywhere from 40-70% of
children with autism have some form of sleep disturbance. It's
important for parents to understand the different types of sleep
problems, and how best to help them.

- **Problems going to sleep** generally occur because of lack of a
  bedtime routine, lack of a specific time to go to bed, or lack
  of a clearly defined sleep location, including both a bedroom
  and a bed. Intermittent problems going to sleep can arise
  from a long daytime nap, fears such as a monster in the dark,
  too much stimulation just before bedtime, or a medication
  side effect.

- **Problems staying asleep** can be caused by falling asleep in
  one location and being transferred to a regular bed, a
  caregiver leaving the room after the child falls asleep,
  needing to eat or drink at night, medical effects, medical
  illness (ear infection), daytime stressors that cause bad
  dreams, or unexpected external noises.

- **Problems with sleep phase** (the time when the child
  normally falls asleep and awakens the next morning) result
  from excessive stimulation, letting a child decide when to go
  to bed, or changes in the Circadian rhythm. Disruptions
  during sleep can be caused by sleepwalking, bed-wetting,
  teeth-grinding, head-banging and night terrors.

Ten strategies to help restore sleep

1. Start a Sleep Diary and document exactly when and how
   often the problems occur.

2. Look for physical problems that can impair sleep.

3. Look for behavior problems that can impair sleep.

4. Set up a regular bedtime routine and stick to it; use visual
   cues or a visual schedule if needed.

5. Avoid excessive stimulation before bed.

6. The child should fall asleep in the location that is meant only for sleep—his bed.

7. Create a sleep environment—quiet, dark, controlled temperature (not too warm), and a comfortable bed and linens.

8. If the child often wanders out of his room, consider gating the doorway or installing a Dutch door with the top open and the bottom locked.

9. Survey the room for disturbing items: clicking clocks, tree limbs that scratch against the window or side of the house, the on/off hum of the heating or cooling unit outside or next door, the feel of the sheets or the pattern.

10. Maintain the same sleep environment when the child is falling asleep as will exist when the child stays asleep or wakes in the middle of the night. That means parents should resist staying in the room until the child falls asleep.

Explaining death to the child with autism. The loss of a relative, friend or pet can leave parents at a loss for how to explain the disappearance of a loved one without unduly frightening their concrete-thinking child. Spiritual concepts of God, heaven, angels and souls may simply fall flat and add to the child's bewilderment. *Lifetimes: The Beautiful Way to Explain Death to Children* by Bryan Mellonie will be imminently useful for such children: "There is a beginning and an ending for everything that is alive. In between there is living," it explains.

The book is a beautiful and sensitive but very concrete discussion of the framing of a life between birth and death, how life spans differ among plants, animals and people, about the markers and touchstones in those lives between birth and death, and about how beginnings and endings are going on around us at all times. It passes no judgments as to what may or may not be "fair" and does not discuss grief or the feeling of loss associated with bereavement, or with spiritual concepts of afterlife.

Change one thing at a time. Many parents fear that time is running out and will often try several different therapies or interventions at the same time. The result? It becomes impossible to determine which intervention is producing a positive change in the child. Is it the new diet, the change in medication, the new sensory therapy or the modified educational program?

Start one thing at a time. In most cases, a short thirty-day trial period is all that is needed between different treatments to observe emerging changes or effects.

Helping the medicine go down. As your child gets older, medications will appear less in liquid form and more in pill form. Don't wait until illness is upon your child to see whether or not he can choke a pill down. Practicing under calm, non-emergency conditions will yield better results. Our pediatrician recommends practicing with a bottle and a non-medicinal item such as M&M's® or mini-M&M's®. Glugging the water out of a bottle instead of sipping from a glass forces the head back and helps the pill go down.

A little more help. And, speaking of medications: Medication costs are skyrocketing. Contact the pharmaceutical company that manufactures the medication(s) your child uses. Many companies have programs to provide free prescriptions for patients in need.

Spray vitamins. So many kids with ASD have limited diets, eating only a handful of different foods. Others have digestive problems that prevent proper absorption of nutrients from foods. A quick and easy way to make sure your child is getting essential vitamins and nutrients is to try a spray vitamin. Just a couple of sprays on the tongue and that's it. No pills for kids to wrestle with swallowing or to spit back out, no added fillers, no need for Mom to crush up the vitamin and or try to hide it in food. Another benefit: spray vitamins enter the child's circulatory system in less than thirty seconds, bypassing the GI track, so more of the good stuff can be utilized by the body. Find manufacturers of spray vitamins via any major Internet search engine.

Preventing ear infections. According to Dr. Stephen M. Edelson, Ph.D., at the Center for the Study of Autism in Salem, Oregon, "several large-scale surveys have shown that ear infections are more frequent in children with developmental delays, autism, and fetal alcohol syndrome." Recurring ear infections can lead to speech and language problems in later years.

"There is mounting evidence," says Dr. Edelson, "that many ear infections, possibly the majority, are primarily a reaction to an allergen. These allergens may be airborne (e.g., pollen, mold, secondhand smoke, dust, animal dander) and/or certain food items. The common food items are: dairy products, wheat, eggs, chocolate, nuts, and sugar."

If you suspect airborne allergens are contributing to your child's chronic ear infections, restrict smoking and pets to areas outside your home. Consider installing a freestanding or furnace filter to kill airborne microorganisms.

If you suspect a food item, such as cow's milk, eliminate it from his diet for a period of several weeks to see if there is any change.

> *Tip*: Eliminate only one food at a time so you can isolate the offending substance.

> *Tip*: If the culprit is a food allergy, it is most likely something he likes and is eating regularly. Taking it away cold turkey may be needlessly upsetting. Weaning your child away from the food item over a period of a week or two is just as effective but much less traumatic. For instance, if it's milk, first substitute out the cheese sandwich at lunch for a non-dairy filling. Then substitute out the ice cream for dessert. Then go from three glasses of milk per day to two. A few days later drop to one, then none.

Medications: be sure to be thorough. You need complete information when a doctor recommends psychotherapeutic medications as part of your child's treatment plan. Some physicians may not disclose all the information they should without your prompting. By asking the following questions, you will better understand the recommended medications:

1. What is the name of the medication? Is it known by other names?

2. How do body systems absorb and eliminate the medication?

3. What do researchers know about the medication's effectiveness in patients, especially those with ASD?

4. How will the medication help my child?

5. How long does it take before we see improvement?

6. What side effects commonly occur? Are there possible serious side effects?

7. Is this medication addictive? Can the child abuse it?

8. What is the recommended dosage? How often will the medication be taken and at what time of day?

9. Are there laboratory tests, such as heart function or blood tests that are needed before taking the medication? Will any tests be required while using the medication?

10. Will a physician monitor my child's response to the medication, making dosage changes if necessary? Who will assess my child's progress and how often?

11. How long will my child need the medication? What factors will lead to a decision to stop this medication?

12. Should my child avoid any other medications or foods while taking the medication?

13. Should my child stop participating in any particular activity while taking the medication?

14. What do we do if a problem develops? For example, what if my child becomes ill, he misses doses, or we see signs of side effects?

15. What is the cost of the medication (generic vs. brand name)? Does health insurance cover it? What sort of financial assistance is available?

16. Do we need to tell the school staff about this medication?

17. Can we get written information about the medication?

Chapter 5

A Sensitive Awareness of Others

Social/Relationship Strategies and Considerations

Manners are a sensitive awareness of the feelings of others. If you have that awareness, you have good manners, no matter what fork you use.

Emily Post

Social stories. Throughout this book you will see references to social stories as a means of facilitating behavior modification, transitions and social understanding. Not a generic term, a Social Story™ is a carefully scripted text that describes a *process* and a *result* in terms that make sense and are applicable to the person with ASD.

A Social Story™ is written based on four sentence types: descriptive (fact-based), perspective (acknowledges feelings or opinions of self and others), directive (suggests acceptable responses or reactions to social situations) and affirmative (why the action or description is good). The range of topics about which a social story can be employed is limitless, and anyone who works with or lives with a child with ASD can write one. Chances are good that your school's autism specialist, speech therapist or psychologist knows about social stories. Consult with them about behavioral, communication, sensory or social skills goals that might be successfully addressed through a social story. Examples: eating at the cafeteria, taking turns on the playground, moving to a new school, riding the bus, visiting the doctor, buying something in a store, acknowledging a favor or gift.

Michigan teacher Carol Gray pioneered the Social Story™ as we know it today in the early 1990s, and her website that is part of The Gray Center for Social Learning and Understanding is excellent. Sample social stories and meticulous guidelines for conceiving and writing social stories are included. For more information visit: http://www.thegraycenter.org/Social_Stories.htm.

A friend indeed. If your child shows an inclination to befriend children a bit younger than himself, encourage it. He may be better able to identify developmentally with a younger child, giving him a sense of social competence he doesn't get from his same-age peers.

Basis of comparison. At home and at school, ensure that his basis of comparison is only to his previous performance, not that of his siblings or classmates.

Encouraging playground interaction. Recess time spent on the playground can be a less-than-desirable activity for many children with autism. Issues relating to noise, environment, teasing or his uncertainty in handling different, often-spontaneous social interactions can be highly stressful for the ASD child. Some children harbor a deep need to be first in line to come in from recess (possibly a personal space issue). They spend the period filled with anxiety and rather than participate in playground activities, hover at the edges of the play area.

Whatever the reasons, teachers and parents can be mindful of these challenges while still providing structure and opportunity for the child to become more comfortable on the playground.

- Change the boundary when returning to class, e.g., enter the building through a different door.

- Bring another child over to interact just a bit, such as showing a ball or asking a question about a topic of interest. If the interaction continues, push it just a bit farther—throw the ball against the wall or into a hoop. Even if the child interacts with the ball only, it is progress.

- If he is used to spending recess in the library instead of on the playground, have him come to the playground just twice a week, and not two days in a row. Allow days when he can still choose the library. Have him participate in working out the schedule of which days will be playground days and which will be library days.

- Pair him up with a peer "buddy" for recess—preferably one who shares some of his favorite interests. Peers can provide the sometimes-needed social instruction without calling attention to the child, as would a teacher's involvement.

- Set up group activities that capitalize on the ASD child's special talents. He gets to share his vast knowledge base and his peers experience him in a positive light.

And speaking of being first in line. Transfer that intense need to be first in line to a positive setting. Would he like to be first to choose a topic for the writing workshop, first to give a speech, first to share his drawing or science project? Try this initially in small groups—speaking to the whole class from the front of the room would give many children, not just the ones with ASD, the frights.

Walk this way. At the same time, the need to be first in line may be telling you something about the child's poor motor planning skills or ability to process vestibular/proprioceptive input. Does the child have difficulty when walking in the middle of the line—does he kick, jab or run into other children, or step on their feet? It is likely he simply needs more space around him when he walks, along with increased awareness of his immediate surroundings. It might help to:

- Place him at the front or the back of the line so he can self-regulate the amount of space around him.

- Have his paraeducator walk in front of him to ensure adequate space.

- Have him carry a heavy object (book/books) close to his chest with his hands holding the opposite arm.

- Have him think of a special song he hums to himself when he walks in line.

- Teach him appropriate protests to use if someone gets too close: "Please move back" or "Please don't touch me."

No two minds are alike. Many of the social nuances that seem to elude a child on the spectrum can be attributed to a lack of Theory of Mind (ToM) skills. ToM involves attributing mental states to others, and more specifically, realizing that people have different ways of thinking and feeling about things. They also have different interests, like and dislikes that impact their thoughts and feelings. Carrying it one step further, ToM involves understanding that these different ways of thinking and feeling produce different behaviors from person to person, and that these behaviors are not always consistent! Sound intricate? Well, it is, and it aptly describes why social understanding, or more specifically the lack thereof, can have such a monumental impact on the lives of these children.

To help develop ToM skills in children with autism, try the following:

- Activities that encourage the child to understand the mental states and emotions of others. When reading a book, discuss facial expressions of the characters as indications of their thoughts; do the same when watching videos or movies. Create games such as "What's He Thinking?" or "What's She Feeling?"—have fun and purposely be silly from time to time to illustrate different mental states.

- Activities that encourage pretend play.

- Activities that enhance perspective-taking. Talk about your thoughts and feelings out loud to your child on a regular basis as an example of a point of view that may be different than his; set up a "Today I Feel _____" board at home or school and have each member actively participate; incorporate Comic Strip Conversations (originated by Carol Gray)—simple drawings used to illustrate conversations between people—as a teaching tool.

- For parents and teachers who want to learn more about Theory of Mind, a good source of information and ideas is the book, *Teaching Children with Autism to Mind-Read: A Practical Guide*, by Howlin, Baron-Cohen and Hadwin (1999).

Peek-a-Boo. The foundations for social relationships are built very early in life. One of the earliest relationship skills that infants develop is called "social referencing." Think back to when your child was very young and he encountered something startling and new. What was his reaction? Neurotypical children will immediately look at Mom or Dad as an information source: Is it safe? Am I in danger? Should I be fearful? Am I okay? They already know, even at six months old, that parents can provide them with valuable clues about the social world around them. In children with autism, social referencing is absent, leaving the child unattached and alone in how he experiences people and events in his earliest, formative years (and beyond, if it is never taught). Parents and preschool teachers can teach social referencing by using some of the ideas that follow. Since this is a foundation skill that many other social skills are built upon, it should be taught to children of any age who do not employ social referencing on their own.

- The goal is to teach the child to reference you as an information source. So any type of game or activity that reinforces this action is ideal for teaching social referencing. Try Peek-a-Boo or Hide and Seek, with exaggerated gestures and exclamations.

- Change play routines mid-stream so the child needs you to show or tell him what to do next.

- Have a child crawl on his belly or hands and knees through a long fabric tunnel or a couple of pup tents aligned end to end. The parent or adult remains at the end, with her face either just inside the end of the tunnel, as a reference point, or playing Peek-a-Boo with the child as he crawls through.

- Back and forth activities, such as rolling a ball along the floor or batting a balloon, require the child to pay attention to his partner's actions.

Do you see what I see? During the toddler year, "joint referencing" emerges in the NT child, another indication of ToM skill development. Witness the exuberant child, who upon seeing a balloon floating in the sky, points to it and looks at Mom to make sure she sees it too. The meaning behind "shared experience"—the feeling of connecting to another human being, is already developing in the child. He is anxious to share his joy and excitement with a parent; he feels the social connection that shared experiences bring.

Pointing is one of the earliest indications that joint referencing is developing in a child. In the absence of pointing, parents can teach a child to feel social connection through the following shared activities and games:

- Timed, synchronized movements the child and adult perform together, especially those that elicit lots of laughter and fun, are ideal activities that give the child a sense of shared experience. Try running together holding hands, falling together, carrying objects together or racing cars side by side. String a variety of different movements together to keep interest levels high.

- Start-stop activities, with each person taking turns as the leader are also effective. Paddle drums and drumsticks, hand clapping, or Simon Says variations work well.

- As skills develop, incorporate more variation and fewer routine actions into the game. Introduce minor, planned disruptions so the child can practice self-regulation of speed, action, voice, etc.

Feeling the connection. Consider what the world may be like for the child who never develops social referencing or experiences the joy of shared experience in her formative years. Each experience she experiences alone. The idea that she can reference Mom or Dad or a sibling for information is missing from her brain's processing. Her only arsenal of knowledge comes from situations she has specifically experienced herself. And, furthermore, her level of understanding suggests to her that all other people around her experience the world in the very same way she does. How limited does her world then become? Each pleasant experience she recalls pleasantly; each fear-filled experience she recalls again with fear. If a situation resulted in difficulty, chaos or defeat, where does she turn to learn an alternative way?

It is no wonder that such children withdraw from the complexities of social situations at an early age. Life is too uncertain; black and white rules governing social interaction are nonexistent. How can a child effectively know what to say or do in any given social situation if he is unable to make sense of another person's behavior?

Steven Gutstein, a pioneer in the field of social relationship development for kids with ASD, outlines in his book, *Autism Asperger's:*

Solving the Relationship Puzzle, a six-level hierarchy for teaching social awareness.

1. Tuning In
2. Learning to Dance
3. Improving and Co-creating
4. Sharing Outside Worlds
5. Discovering Inside Worlds
6. Binding Selves to Others

Awareness is the first step in providing our children the fundamental knowledge of social relationships that has been missing for them up until now. Teaching rote social skills is not enough; important, yes, but not enough. We must also teach our children to feel the sense of connection between humans, the exquisite joy that comes through shared feelings and shared understanding. Without that feeling of connection, social skills teaching becomes little more than rote repetition of a sequence of actions; functional in one specific situation but probably not transferable. By concentrating on helping our children feel social connection, we equip them with the inner motivation for life-long social learning to take place that is functional, transferable, compatible and far more emotionally satisfying.

Kelso's Choices. Kelso's Wheel of Choices is a widely used conflict-management curriculum that can help your child deal with the minor conflicts that invariably arise in interpersonal communication. Included with the program is Kelso's Wheel, a concrete, easy to understand visual giving children nine options (arranged in a nonagon) to try when disagreement erupts between children. Children are encouraged to:

- Go to another game
- Share and take turns
- Talk it out
- Walk away

- Ignore it
- Tell the person to stop
- Apologize
- Make a deal
- Wait and cool off

The choices end with instructions to tell a trusted adult if confronted with a BIG problem. What is a BIG problem? A big problem is: 1) a situation where someone might get hurt, 2) a law or an important rule is being broken, or 3) something frightening is happening.

Kelso is an anthropomorphic frog; if this is a turn-off for your child, consider substituting photographs of your child or his siblings or friends enacting the various options. Call it Evan's Wheel of Choice instead. Print the wheel on a card small enough to keep in his desk for reference. Even better, ask your child's teacher or principal to adopt Kelso's Choices as a classroom or school-wide guideline.

Kelso's Choices, Conflict Management for Children, is a product of Rhinestone Press, P.O. Box 30, Winchester, OR 97495, (503) 672-3826.

Custom board game. Logical progression of thoughts, perspective-taking and an appreciation of beginning/middle/ending are all thought processes that impact social skill development. An interesting and fun way to teach these concepts to your child is to create customized board games.

Start by drawing a blank board game with squares in a path, like Candyland. Have your child (with your help if he needs it) invent a game and write into each square an instruction. Roll dice to advance pieces. The path can be across a distance, across time or depict a process.

- Start in your hometown and end in a place you'd like to visit
- Start in kindergarten and end in high school
- Start in the wading pool and end up on the high dive
- Start in Little League and end up as Cal Ripken
- Start with flour, eggs and sugar and end up with a cake
- Start with lemons, water, cups and quarters and end up with a lemonade stand (or other small business)

What's that tune? If you are using a Social Story™ to establish a certain behavior or routine, setting it to music may help the child commit it to memory.

Those who can, teach. Everyone is good at something. Ask your child to teach you something he or she excels at that you may not. Does she have a natural golf swing? Make up her own songs? Role reversal that puts them in charge is empowering.

Guidelines for encouraging play skills. Play is a universal action; kids in all countries and within all cultures play. While play skills may comes naturally to the NT child, many of the social/interpersonal facets of play need to be taught to the child with ASD. Any strategies developed for kids with ASD should include the following key areas:

- Connect and engage—get their attention and make a personal connection
- Motivate—get them to want to be with their peers and participate
- Structure and practice—help them learn the conventional aspects of play through preparation, practice and support
- Include—gradual, planned and well-supported inclusion into groups and the community

Friend to friend. While teaching your child or student the social skills involved with making and keeping friends, enlist the help of her peers too. Kids are generally eager to help a friend or classmate when they understand how best to do it. Start by sharing these basic friendship tips with the child's NT classmates:

- Get your friend's attention before saying anything else: Say your friend's name or position yourself in front of her.
- Use short sentences and small gestures.
- Give choices of activities you know interest him.
- Be like a detective: Watch your friend to see what interests him, upsets him, makes him nervous or stressed out.
- Ask your friend to talk, to join in a game, to come visit; include him.
- Use friendly words and gestures: Tell your friend when she has done something you like.
- Accept differences: We're all good at something and not so good at other things.

When the Mad Hatter comes to play. It's often a stretch of the imagination for young girls with ASD to enjoy a tea party with imaginary food and imaginary guests. Here are a few tips to expand your little princess' pretend play skills.

- Start concretely. Set up a real tea party with real food and drinks. Put the table someplace special and different; use the itty-bitty tea set. Pour out real juice and put real snacks on the plates (bite size, of course).
- Move to toy food. Invite your little one to participate in a tea party with realistic toy food; pretend to eat. Having your learner do the "pouring" and choosing the food will make it even more fun for them. Enjoy your pretend food with exaggerated eating and drinking noises. Work on appropriate language and social skills, too.
- Imaginary food. Have the tea party, but now pretend that there is food on your plate, and beverage in your cup, when there isn't any. Talk about how the food tastes and what you're pretending to drink. Enjoy your imaginary food with

exaggerated eating and drinking noises. Remember to be polite!

- Imaginary friends. (This step can be worked on at the same time as the second and third targets.) Teach your little one to offer food and beverages to stuffed animals and dolls/action figures attending the party. Encourage her to feed the dolls or animals and treat them as if they were real.

- Pretending with real friends. Hold a tea party with one or a few of your child's friends. Encourage your young one to offer imaginary food and beverages to her friends; allow your interaction to fade so typical play can take place.

Choosing toys. It can often be a challenge to find a toy that appeals to the literal-thinking mind of your child with ASD. Before hauling off yet another brainstorm to Goodwill, consider the following:

- Don't pay attention to the ages listed by the manufacturers (except for choking hazards); if it works for your child, it works.

- If a toy does not appeal to your child at first, try it again at a later date. Maybe that sing-along video that didn't even get a second look at two will be well-received at four.

- Think your child is beyond a toy now? Try it again in a few years. There may be different aspects of a toy that appeal at different developmental stages.

- Try the old standbys: Candyland, puzzles, books, CDs. Try jigsaw puzzles made from foam letters with different textured surfaces, or Spell-A-Puzzle™ (International Playthings: 800.445.8347) that combines pictures, letters and words. When you put together the word puzzle, you also create the corresponding picture of the object spelled.

Adaptation. Board games reinforce social skills such as turn-taking, and many are great vocabulary builders as well. Try some of these simple modifications to a few of the more common games to make your ASD child's experience more fun for him, and therefore, the rest of his family.

- PICTIONARY. Allow the child to bypass words he doesn't know, or remove them from the deck beforehand and add your own cards with words known to be in his vocabulary. He can't draw a silo if he doesn't know what it is but he could draw a barn or a farmhouse.

- OUTBURST. Make your own category cards based on her interests (animals we see at the zoo, flavors of ice cream, crayon colors); reduce category items from ten to five; extend or eliminate response time.

- SCRABBLE. Limit everyone to two-syllable common-usage words, allow the child to exchange letters at will, don't keep score.

- MEMORY GAME. Make your own sets of matching cards using a camera and a color copier. Instead of jungle animals, etc. use family members, classmates, his Matchbox car collection, her Beanie Babies.

- With other games: Consider starting the game with pieces halfway to the finish to help kids with short attention spans interact positively.

Good trade. The concept of sharing toys is difficult even for NT children but can be nearly impossible for the child who identifies with only a few classroom items. If the word "sharing" sets off firestorms, 1) call it something else and 2) place a tolerable but gradually increasing time parameter on it. Call it a trade, an exchange, a swap, a switch. Set a timer so the child knows when he can have his original item back. Make the initial time brief so he can gain confidence in the process. Gradually increase swap time.

"Trading" as opposed to "sharing" also implies that the child gets something in return for giving up his item. It is reciprocal, and it eliminates the open-ended quality of "sharing" that can be so distressing.

Identifying emotions. Recognizing, acknowledging and understanding emotions, whether in himself or in others, is a core skill in interpersonal relationships. Yet, one of the hallmarks of autism spectrum disorders is an impairment in this area. Kids with ASD often cannot identify the different emotions that make up the human condition, nor do they appreciate that people have different responses, involving different emotions, than he or she might feel in a similar situation.

Emotions and empathy are social skills that will need to be taught to your child or student with ASD. Various books and visual tools are available on the market to help with this. Here are a few suggestions you can employ easily and quickly.

- Take pictures of your child, and some classmates if possible, play-acting different emotions. Let them really ham it up. If your child isn't expressive himself (many kids with autism aren't), then just use the classmates, or family members. Avoid adults, though; you want to use similar aged kids.

- Use the photos to help your child or student "read" the expressions on other people's faces and interpret how it pertains to their feelings. Mindy looks excited here, Nathan looks mad. Julia is feeling silly, Evan is feeling scared. Kelsey looks embarrassed, Henry looks proud.

- If your child doesn't show an interest in his classmates' faces, photos of just the child himself may be the place to start.

- Model the vocabulary of emotion in your everyday conversation with your child or student. Are you *nervous* about a presentation you have to give at work today? Are you *confused* about whether or not your mother wants to go shopping? Are you feeling *disappointed, skeptical* or *confident*? Use words for feelings as frequently as you can.

- Draw her attention to the emotions of other people you encounter within social settings: Play a game in guessing what another person is feeling by his facial expression.

- Point out the physical facial characteristics that clue you to which emotion is being expressed. See the wide-open eyes, his crinkly nose, or how his mouth and cheeks are all scrunched together? Discuss in detail what appears obvious to you. If it were obvious to the child with ASD, he'd be able to pick it up himself.

- Use commercially available "emotions" products that help kids connect facial expressions and emotions. Two good ones to start with: Gaining Face (http://ccoder.com/GainingFace), ethnic-friendly software that helps kids identify emotions, and *How Do I Feel?* by Joan Green (www.greenhousepub.com). The book contains colorful peel-off Velcro® faces that kids insert into sentences describing different emotions in various situations.

The art of questioning. Knowing how to ask a question in order to obtain more information is a skill you may take for granted, particularly if you have a child or student who batters you with an endless barrage of questions. But many children on the autism spectrum do not know how to ask a question. And even when they master the art of formulating their thoughts into intelligible questions, it can take a tremendous amount of courage to get that question out in front of a group.

The art of questioning should be taught and practiced from a young age.

- Games like Lotto ("Who has the bear?"), Go Fish ("Do you have any threes?") or Guess My Name ("Are you an animal? Are you a food?") are good starters.
- Build guessing games into your daily routine. If you bring home a bag of groceries, have your child guess what's in the bag. Is it for breakfast? Is it for dessert? Is it cereal? Is it eggs? Is it oatmeal? Is it cornflakes?
- For classroom or home: make a Mystery Box. Children have to guess what's inside, gradually narrowing down the choices. Start with the category: Is it animals, clothes, food, toy? Then get more specific: Is it brown, is it white, is it red? Do you wear it on the top part of your body or the bottom?

Do you wear it at night or during the day? Winter or summer? And so on.

• With a very young child, take turns playing "What Is It?" with a picture book. Point to an object on the page and ask "What is it?" Turn the page and now it is the child's turn to ask you, "What is it?" This builds vocabulary at the same time it reinforces the habit of asking a question if there is something they do not know or understand.

Look into my crystal ball. Watching a movie or video (one they haven't seen before) with the sound turned off is a great exercise in perception, prediction and querying. What do you think is happening? Look at the characters' faces—are they happy with what's going on? Scared? Worried? Are they friends or do they not like each other? What do you think will happen next?

Stop the movie or story and have the child write or make up his own ending. The task of predicting an event or a sequence of events will be very hard for a child who likes everything black and white. Predicting is an elevated form of guessing, and a necessary skill later in life.

Practice asking for help. It's one of the Catch-22 aspects of autism: Kids often don't know how to act within social situations, causing frustration and stress, yet asking for help is a skill they need to be taught. Phrases like "I don't understand," "Could you repeat that?" or "I need help with this" will not come easily to your child. Let him know that it is okay, and *necessary*, to ask for help, and give him several examples of how to do so.

Asking for help can seem like such a big skill to learn that it may easily go unnoticed that the child has not only mastered the skill, but has, in fact, become *too* dependent upon the teacher or paraeducator. When this happens, it is time to begin helping the student learn to take visual cues from peers or to first ask a peer. Tell him that when he isn't sure what to do, before he asks the teacher he should look around at others at his table or near his desk: Ask your neighbor, "What page are we on?" or "What are we supposed to do?" If you still don't understand, then raise your hand to ask the teacher.

This step will be particularly important for the child who frequently seems oblivious to his environment. He's the one who is still at his desk after everyone else has lined up for recess. But he ultimately has as much, if not more, to learn from his peers than from the teacher; cooperative learning is critical and a skill he'll use throughout his life.

The appropriate protest. You've seen it a thousand times— the pursed lips, the abject refusal, the running away, the head shaking back and forth at warp speed, accompanied by shrieks of "no! no! NO!" Or, it might take the form of a complete shut-down or, conversely, physically aggressive behavior like hitting or biting. What's at issue here is the child who hasn't learned to say "no" in a socially appropriate manner.

Equip your child with more socially appropriate ways to protest than just overt behavior or the emphatic "NO!" Try "I don't know," "I don't want to," "I don't like that," or suggest walking away without verbalizing. For the limited speaking or nonverbal child teach him to use a simple hand gesture for "Stop," or provide him with a communication card he can use.

I need a break. If the student can indicate, in appropriate ways, when he needs a break from social interaction, an important step in self-regulation has been achieved. It can be as simple as telling you, "I need a break" or handing you a "Break" card (make sure you teach him how and when to use it beforehand). A self-regulation break is just that—a break to regroup, regain a sense of calm, and then return to the activity or interaction. Don't call it a time-out, which may have punitive connotations.

A break can be as simple as going to the water foundation, even if he is not thirsty. A reading corner with a basket of hand fidgets helps many children regroup. Or, create a "Sensory Space"—a dedicated room designed with sensory needs in mind, for children who need to regroup in more major ways. However self-regulation breaks are implemented, they help further the child's ability to be successful in daily interactions with the people around him.

Conversational listening. Help your child learn how to be a listener. Teach her the social cues that are associated with listening: to look at the person who is talking to her, nod her head, make a rejoinder comment. The rejoinder can be as simple as "Wow!" or "That's cool"—anything that indicates to the speaker that he has been heard. Explain to her that conversational listening involves more than just her. At first, she may not understand why, if she knows she is listening, she needs to let the person who is talking also know she is listening. Also, give your child a personal-space guideline: When speaking to someone, keep an arm's length away. Many kids with ASD are chronic "space invaders."

Time to say goodbye. Saying goodbye puts an end bracket on a conversation. In our culture, merely walking away at the end of sentence is considered rude or awkward. Teaching your child how to say goodbye doesn't have to mean using those exact words. Goodbye can be "See you later," "Hasta la vista!" or "It was nice talking to you." For the not-yet verbal child, it can be a wave, a nod, a smile. Brainstorm with your child the different ways of saying goodbye and then practice often and in different ways.

Chapter 6

Learners and Doers

Teaching and Education Strategies and Considerations

You are all learners, doers and teachers.

Richard Bach

R-E-S-P-E-C-T. Nearly every professional interviewed for this book emphasized the importance of not talking about the child in front of him, even when "catching" him at something good. Rather than letting him overhear you telling the teacher, "Jacob did a great job on his math sheet," tell him directly: "Jacob, you did a great job on your math sheet." Or, ask his permission to tell a third party: "Jacob, may I tell Mrs. Porter what a great job you did on your math sheet?"

Look twice. When a first-grader with autism was observed frequently putting his hands over his ears, his teacher assumed the problem was noise. Upon closer observation, an OT discovered that it wasn't always—sometimes the child was pressing deeply on his cheekbones and temples, indicating a sensory invasion other than noise. His teacher was then able to pinpoint other irritations—kids crowding in line around him or glare from the window that was affecting his sensory systems.

Two is better than one. If she constantly falls behind in homework because of forgetting to bring home her textbook, ask that an extra one be issued to keep at home. If the school cannot issue one, look for a used copy online.

All that noise! Hearing sensitivity is the most commonly reported sensory processing difficulty for individuals with autism. Felt or tennis balls put on the legs of chairs and desks can help minimize noise within a classroom or at home.

Lamb Chop's report card. As you attempt to teach social-emotional skills to your students with ASD, have your students create report cards for characters in a favorite book. They can rate the skill level of the characters in various social arenas: helping others, empathy, self-motivation, daily interpersonal skills, manners, etc.

Focus, focus. Visual and auditory stimuli can often be distracting to students who need to focus on an in-class assignment. A solution is to have students create portable desk-top or floor-standing privacy screens they can use whenever they need to shut out the rest of the class. The screens can be used by all kids, not just kids with ASD.

Listen up. Where there is more than one teacher in the classroom, designate only one to give instructions for each task or project. Students with ASD yearn for routine and consistency; many voices create opportunities for misunderstanding and challenge their already overtaxed auditory systems. A few tips for verbal instructions follow:

- Use as few words as possible. Instructions that are too wordy will be lost in translation, as will instructions that are repeated by more than one adult but with slight variations.

- If the child appears not to understand the instructions, rephrase using fewer words.

- Opt for positive phrasing rather than negative. Some children with ASD hear only the final verb. Example: A child is climbing too high on the playground equipment and jumping off. The child may hear only the last word of "Don't jump"—and jumps. For this child, it may be better to say "Please climb down."

Keep cultures in mind. Allow extra teaching time to compensate for cultural or socioeconomic factors that further disadvantage a child with ASD. If you are teaching keyboard skills to a child who does not have a computer at home, there is no outlet for home practice and more time must be provided at school or in an after-school instructional setting.

Small group versus large group. Break classroom activities into small groups wherever possible. The child with autism may find the whole-group classroom intimidating or overwhelming; she is then less likely to participate and more likely to simply recede into the background. The same child might succeed with the same material in a smaller group, where each child has a defined role and responsibility. Mixed ability groups mean everyone learns from each other, too.

Review tests. If tests are being administered to determine services for your child, or as a basis for grades in the classroom, ask to see the test. Be comfortable that the test is really measuring what it claims to measure and speak up if you are not sure that it does, especially if it is going to affect placement or therapies rendered.

> *Example*: A Functional Communication Assessment we saw recently for a ten-year-old boy with autism noted that, in the Word-R Test, "he had the most difficulty when asked to change a semantic absurdity such as '*Mark quit the football team because he was a poor batter.*'" This sentence is not a test of semantics, it is a test of sports knowledge. The child being tested had no background in or exposure to football. If the sentence had been, "*Mark put his coat on to go swimming,*" the child in question likely would have responded with, "That's silly!"

New school? Plan ahead. Transitioning to a new school, especially from preschool to elementary school, can be a frightening experience. New teachers, new kids, new routines—lots of places for mishaps and miscues to occur that can quickly erode your child's self-esteem. With a little planning and thought, parents can help kids pre-learn skills that will contribute to daily success.

Ask your child's teacher for a "map" of what his day will involve, then practice skills at home that might prevent unanticipated problems: taking off his coat and hanging it on a hook, using a pencil sharpener or eraser, concentrating when it's less than quiet, walking with a cafeteria tray, opening and closing a lunch box or bag, handling a sandwich baggie, juice box or other implements, throwing the trash away properly, etc.

Visit the new school, the new teacher and the new classroom before the first day. Take photos of his new surroundings: the classroom, the gym, the playground, the lunchroom. Also take photos of the new people with whom he will come in contact: the classroom teacher and educational assistants, the principal, the school secretary, the librarian, the PE teacher, the music teacher, the resource teacher, the school cook, custodian, bus driver. Ask to see the class roster in order to identify a few friends who will also be in your child's class. Use the photos to construct a Social Story™ that emphasizes the things he noticed and liked on his visit: "I will get to play on the spiral slide." "Roger and Lisa will sit near me in class." End the story with an affirmation: "I will like my new school."

The driver on the bus says . . . . Ask yourself how much autism training your child's regular bus driver has received, and the answer will probably be "not a whole heck of a lot." Yet, the driver is responsible for your child under circumstances that are often high-anxiety and sensory laden: the noise from the kids, the stops and starts, the hot and cold temperatures, the fumes, the bullies.

Parents or teachers can help make the ride easier for everyone by creating a Driver Tip Sheet that lists important information about a child and how best to communicate with him. Include his photo, a short positive description of the child, his likes (reinforcers) and dislikes, a list of simple strategies that work with him and some activities that can be done on the bus that will keep the child's interest.

Avoid teaching compliance. Finding the source of behaviors can be tricky business. Teachers who have marginal experience working with the ASD population can easily misinterpret behaviors that occur as a result of one of the underlying challenges of the disorder—sensory issues, social misunderstanding, communication difficulties—as noncompliance, i.e., the student's unwillingness to comply with instructions. When faced with a behavior that remains unchanged despite their best efforts, teachers may request that a behavior specialist step in and create a plan to extinguish the noncompliant behavior. It may work, but then what happens? Usually another behavior problem emerges.

While the idea—avoiding teaching compliance and looking for root causes of behavior—may sound simple, it is actually a very integral part of effective teaching in working with students with ASD and one that is, sadly, often disregarded. When a child's problematic behavior doesn't change, it means the teaching *does* need to change. Something has been overlooked. Behavior is always communication, and in 90% of behavior challenges with autism, compliance is not the issue at hand. Learn to be a good behavior detective.

Fire Drills—Red Alert. For some children with ASD, the sudden violent noise of a fire alarm will send them into a full-blown meltdown. The sound can be extremely painful to the student, and the resulting commotion can push them over the edge. If your child has sensitive hearing, work with the child's teacher to determine how best to handle fire drills. The child may need to be told exactly when the fire drill will occur. For others, knowing the fire drill is coming may cause them to obsess while waiting for it. This child may be better off being given a more general warning: "Remember the fire drill we practice sometimes? We are going to get to do that again today but I am not exactly sure when." No matter what works best, just make sure you've planned for it ahead of time.

Slow-mo. Adapt some play games for a child with motor skill coordination challenges by using a half-dead battery to slow down the motion.

Reluctant/disinterested reader. A child who shows no interest in typical children's books may be very interested in reading his own material. Have him write out his stories or narratives and read them back to you. If he doesn't write yet, he can dictate them to you. Write them out neatly or type them up and read them back to him.

Touch and learn. Three-dimensional tracing of numerals and letters may help the student with space/ground difficulties. Form thick letters with white or colored glue and allow them to dry. Have the student trace each letter with his finger: starting point, direction, end point.

Teach one skill at a time. Mastering a "mature pencil grip" and learning how much pressure needs to be applied when using a pencil are major tasks for sensory-challenged students. Learning to form numerals and letters at the same time is yet another difficult pairing.

Break apart the skills and practice them independently of one another. Offer alternative ways of learning related skills. For instance, let him practice numerals and letters with a felt pen (little pressure required), and practice pencil grip and pressure with shapes, squiggles and less precise requirements.

A desktop or floor-standing easel provides a different writing angle and may help with both motor skills and hand-eye coordination. Make your own lined paper if the child requires wider spacing than on commercially available products.

Stay on the lines. Some kids on the autism spectrum have visual processing challenges that make writing letters along a line a very difficult task. Try using raised-line paper: wide-ruled paper with a raised line to help the child stay on track. Available through Magical Toys and Products: www.magicaltoysandproducts.com.

Fine motor warm up. Some children may need to release tension in their hands in order to start or complete a fine motor task. Provide them with a squeeze ball to use as a warm up and/or throughout the task. Or have him shake his hands, or clench and unclench them. For more fun, pair it with a song or music.

Reduce the glare. Many white papers produce a glare that is painful for light-sensitive eyes. (Notice that all copier papers now carry a "brightness" rating?) Using soft gray, pastel-colored or off-white paper may help. Ditto for the ink color. Black may be too stark. Try a softer color.

Lighting option. Fluorescent tubes that reflect up instead of down greatly reduce visual vibration.

The Tao of choosing an educational program. When choosing a program for your child, remember to look from results backward, not from theory forward. Start with a discussion of what you want your child to be able to do, then work backward to the instructional model or intervention method that best matches his or her learning style.

Eyes wide open. Use exaggerated gestures and expressions when teaching a concept; it helps promote language comprehension. Plus, the visual gesture or visual expression reinforces learning. Stop! (hand extended, palm forward), Oops! (eyes wide, hand over mouth), Up, etc.

Participation Plans. A Participation Plan is a one-page sheet that describes how a student with ASD takes part in a given activity. For example, a plan may explain how a nonverbal student participates in circle time, using a video output device programmed by a peer, where to position the device, and what natural cues or prompts the student needs to communicate using the device. It can even include alternative strategies if the device is unavailable.

A student may have one or several Participation Plans, depending on the number of daily activities that need modification. Each plan 1) describes the typical activity; 2) summarizes related IEP goals; 3) explains special preparation, strategies and materials, including where they are located; 4) shows how the student participates at each step; 5) indicates alternative activities, if appropriate.

Prioritize plans according to need, beginning with plans for the most frequent or frustrating activities, and keep them well organized in a binder. Share plans with all staff who work with the child, especially substitutes, interns or volunteers. As a child progresses, review and revise plans.

Fluency/precision teaching. Fluency strategies are designed to take an existing skill and increase accuracy and speed of skill performance in order to develop competence. For example, a child may be able to tell someone his name ten seconds after being asked, but if he's already lost the attention of the person asking, that skill isn't going to help his social success.

Precision Teaching literature suggests that teaching a skill fluently (achieving accuracy plus speed as a requirement of mastery) achieves the following goals: 1) retention, 2) endurance: the skill can be performed at a particular level over time, and 3) application: the ability to combine elements of a behavior to create a more sophisticated behavior.

Fluency experts claim that when maintenance skills are taught to fluency, it eliminates the need to keep revisiting maintenance tasks to ensure that they aren't lost.

Teaching a Skill to Fluency
- Choose a target skill. Be specific: teaching math is too general; teaching prime numbers is better.

- Define the goal. Your initial goal might be to have the child identify the prime numbers from 1-20.

- Teach the skill. Take time; teach the skill using learning strategies that work for the particular child.

- Select a fluency target rate. Once the skill is acquired, select a rate of responding or performance standard that would help the child achieve retention, endurance, and application. There are no norms for performance standards; they change over time and between learners. Performance standards are short for most skills (e.g., one response every second for fifteen to thirty seconds). Math skills can be targeted at rates ranging from eightyto one hundred digits per minute. Responses that take more sophisticated processing, like reading, can also be performed over one minute intervals.

- Shorter response times can produce better results, according to professionals. In some cases, a ten-second fluency burst can be more effective than a thirty-second fluency burst. Don't push the learner into fatigue either with the number or length of fluency bursts.

Help for the substitute teacher. Resources that can help a substitute teacher quickly learn about the students she will be teaching are invaluable. A Student Profile for each child with ASD in your class is a helpful way to share a snapshot understanding of the students. A Profile should be short—one page is best—and could contain:

- A photo of the student.
- Strengths and challenges.
- Dominant learning style.
- Special learning needs or assistive equipment.
- Brief summary of major IEP goals currently being worked on.
- Key contact information.

Keep all the Student Profiles in a binder, along with other pertinent information: the class daily schedule, a map of the school, the discipline policy, emergency response plan, etc. Be sure to check your school's policies on the confidentiality of student information when implementing this.

Produce and progress. Organizing a child's environment can facilitate learning and skill development. Put that philosophy to work in your classroom. Set up a work basket or box for the child that contains tasks that must be completed before taking a break. Number the projects 1, 2, 3 to let the child know which to do first, second and third. Teach the child how to use the work basket, and ensure that the child knows where to put completed work. A separate box works for some; for others a folder or just a different spot is all that's needed. The break at the end of the work period should be something desirable to the child: a short walk, computer time, drawing time, a snack. This simple process enhances the child's ability to work independently, promoting self-esteem and a sense of accomplishment.

Two red cars + two red cars. Use a child's interests to create a custom set of math manipulatives. This could be little barrettes, plastic ponies or dinosaurs, Matchbox cars, baseball cards, shells, rocks, or doll shoes. If the items don't all match, so much the better—they can be sorted, compared, patterned and made into story problems.

Selecting a keyboard font. When teaching a child with autism to keyboard, a serif font (such as **Times New Roman**) is generally a better choice than a sans serif font (such as **Arial**). Serifs are the little tags or tails on the letters of certain type fonts. Sans serif fonts, with their clean straight lines may make it difficult for the child to distinguish between an upper case I and a lower case L. According to typographers, serif fonts are more readable, as they appear to lead the eye across the line of type.

> *Tip:* The most difficult-to-read text is that which is set all in capital letters. That's why it's used sparingly and only for short sentences or phrases. Our minds learn to visually process words not only by their individual letters, but also by the shape of the word itself. To read a word in capital letters, our minds need to slow down and individually process each letter, one at a time.

What happened at school today? It's the No.1 question parents usually ask their child at the end of every school day. Yet, many parents of children with ASD receive either no response or get little in the way of useful, concrete information. The solution is to create a Communication Book, a simple handmade book that goes back and forth from home to school with the child each day. It lets Mom know what went on at school that day and helps a teacher by letting her know what has happened at home since she last saw the student.

Keep the book simple and small enough to easily fit into a child's backpack. A half-page format works well. Create a simple form and photocopy pages, adding/replacing as needed. The "Notes from Home" page is filled out by the parent each morning; the teacher completes the Notes from School page just prior to the end of the school day. A sample form follows.

NOTES FROM HOME   DATE:_____

Last night I _____slept well   _____didn't sleep well   why?_____

Today I am feeling
____happy _____sad ____sleepy ____frustrated ____just OK ____well rested

Note from parent (special instructions, interesting experience):
_____
_____

Ask Julia about (something that happened after school that she wants to share):
_____
_____

Please call today. Phone number and best time to call: _____

NOTES FROM SCHOOL   DATE:_____

Today at school I was ____happy _____sad ____sleepy ____frustrated ____just OK

Activities today: ____library ____PE ____music ____assembly __other:_____ :

Art:
_____

Science/Social studies:
_____

Math:
_____

Books/reading:
_____

This week we are studying/working on:
_____

Special Notes/Questions:_____

Introducing new subjects to the child with limited interests.

He's interested only in trains and outer space; how do you engage his interest in curriculum areas outside his limited range, such as the human body or the Oregon Trail? First, understand why his interests are so limited: He does what is familiar and comfortable within the limitations of his sensory, social and language deficits. Then:

- Rather than making the new subject the entry point, expose the child to the new subject through his interest area. Start where self-motivation is high and he has already excelled.

  ~ Connect the two areas: What constellations would the pioneers have seen in the summer sky during the journey on the Oregon Trail? What engines types were used in the first transcontinental railroads? How did the building of the railroads affect the wagon trains?

  ~ Compare and contrast the two areas: In what ways are a journey on the Oregon Trail and a voyage to Mars different? In what ways are they alike? How are an engine and a human body alike or different— what are their parts, their fuel, how fast do they go, what sorts of "illnesses" do they get (boiler sludge versus chest colds)?

- Develop language objectives for the unit as well as content objectives. Don't assume a level of vocabulary he may not have: Barrel, oxen, blacksmith and settler are not words commonly occurring in 21st century kid-conversation.

- Focus more on comprehension than on content. Understanding the impact of the steam engine on the country's development is a more useful bit of knowledge than is learning specific dates of various events that occurred along the way, isn't it? Support with props, pictures, concrete objects.

- Show enthusiasm for your subject! It's contagious. The child will sense if you are only mildly interested in the subject yourself.

The learning triangle. The Reggio Emelia approach to education contains many principles that are highly pertinent to teaching children with autism spectrum disorders. The overreaching philosophy is that the classroom environment is the child's third teacher, along with the parents and the teacher. (For more information visit:

http://www.cmu.edu/cyert-center/rea.htm). The ideas that follow are suggestions for making the classroom environment friendlier for the child with autism (and his peers too!).

Bring the outdoors inside. Our very resourceful occupational therapist does an exercise where she asks the staff and children in the special education classroom to tell her about their favorite memory from childhood, and to draw a picture of it. Then the memories are shared together. She has found that almost all of the time, favorite memories occur outdoors. They then talk about the "richness" of the environment and its sensory experiences.

Teachers: Create a classroom environment everyone will love. Use these great ideas to bring the outdoors inside!

- Use natural, seasonal items for math manipulatives: acorns, pinecones, pebbles, seed pods. These items provide visual and tactile interest that plastic items simply cannot.
- Suspend a large branch from the ceiling as a natural canopy. Add "found" items like abandoned bird nests.
- Have plants in the room (nontoxic of course). Large floor plants and hanging spider plants work well.
- Remove fluorescent lighting and replace with "natural light" tubes.
- A small indoor waterfall or foundation can be a soothing background sound.
- Frame children's artwork in simple natural wood frames that the kids make themselves. Have kids break twigs into same sized lengths and glue them around a simple wooden frame; use grapevine tendrils for a more "artsy" look.
- Pressed, laminated leaves can be hung mobile-style from the ceiling.
- Make leaf prints, flower prints or fish prints.

The kids in our OT's classroom named forts, spider webs and jungle huts as their favorite outdoor places. Their teacher constructed a jungle hut arrangement in a corner of the class. The kids could go there to "hide" (self-regulate) when they needed a break, and it opened a whole ongoing discussion on homes for both people and animals (the spider web being the spider's home). Interestingly, the class expressed no fear of spiders, just a pronounced fascination with webs.

Reduce clutter. Rule #1: Reduce clutter. Rule #2: Reduce clutter. Rule #3: Reduce clutter. Teachers tend to be natural collectors. Because budgets are tight and replacement materials are hard to come by, they hang onto oodles of stuff because they might need it someday. Clutter and disorder is very visually distracting for children with ASD and makes it difficult for them to move smoothly from activity to activity. Try to limit storage in the classroom to items used on a daily, weekly or monthly basis. Find another space for longer-term storage.

Lost in space? Children with autism can be self-limiting in their interests and, therefore, in how they utilize the different areas of the classroom. They frequently get locked into a certain interest area or they don't feel comfortable with open-ended activities. A twenty-minute "mini-study" will enlighten you as to how you might better involve a student in classroom activities. Have a parent or other adult assistant do the study for you. Make a quick drawing of the room and with a colored pen make an X to represent the child at his starting place. Then just draw a line indicating where he goes for the next twenty minutes. Do a second chart with a different colored pen for another child, or several children. You'll probably see that the child with ASD only utilizes a small portion of the room, and it might not be much different for some of his neuro-typical peers. Think about how the room could be changed strategically so that the children can do multiple things at one location. Example: Place a block area next to a science area, with materials that can be moved/shared between the two activities.

> *Tip*: Move activity areas away from the walls, away from the perimeter of the room. Doing so encourages exploration as kids walk through different areas during their

day. Being forced to move diagonally rather than in a straight path through the room encourages attention and awareness.

These four walls. Colorful posters, fancy character alphabets and other generic classroom wall art may be cute but are often visually overwhelming for the child with ASD. Limit wall displays to items that are truly meaningful to the students:

- Framed or matted artwork from each child (have a quote from each child under their art), that is changed on a monthly basis
- The week's vocabulary words
- Photos of the children doing various school activities
- A visual schedule of the day's routine

You'll know if your classroom displays are meaningful if a parent could walk into the room when no one's around and still get "echoes" of the children who bring that space to life during the day. It should feel personal and welcoming.

> *Tip:* Walls should be of a neutral color, or just one color, so as not to compete with or draw focus away from the information on the wall. Soft colors are less energetic— a help for students with visual processing difficulties. However, show caution in using yellow—it's the most frequently cited color that negatively affects individuals on the spectrum.

Light me up. Lighting has an enormous effect on children with autism. Fluorescent lighting has been shown over and over again to be a major problem. First, it produces a low hum that can be very disturbing to their hypersensitive hearing. On top of that, the pulsing nature of the light can distort their visual perception, making objects and people in the room appear to be in constant movement. There are many ways to modify the lighting in your classroom:

- Replace fluorescent tubes with newer, natural light simulating tubes. This reduces flickering.

- Provide the child with autism with an incandescent lamp on his desk. This will also reduce the flickering of the fluorescents.

- Maximize use of daylight in the classroom, but watch for glare and sharp surface reflections. Blinds and shades can help direct light.

- Turn off some (half) of the overhead fluorescent lighting. It may still be enough for classroom work.

- Supplement reduced fluorescent lighting with incandescent floor lamps.

- Think about providing a study carrel (or two) in the room with an incandescent desk lamp. Any student needing to shut out visual distractions to increase focus on his or her work can use it. It can be an important step toward self-regulation.

First-then rather than if-then. Use a "first-then" strategy to phrase instructions, rather than "if-then." Example: "First we will put the paints away (or do our math problems), then we will go out to the playground." Rather than: "If you clean up your mess, then you can go to recess." First-then instructions suggest sequencing and appeal to the logical-thinking patterns of ASD kids. If-then strategies imply a conditional attainment of a goal, often creating unnecessary performance-related stress.

Seeing time. Time can be a nebulous concept for children who think in visual pictures. Giving the child a timer is an effective, concrete way of letting him know the starting and stopping times for a given activity or task. A kitchen timer, stopwatch or wrist watch with an alarm works well. In the classroom or at home, try a device called the Time Timer. The general principle is the same as a kitchen timer, but time is depicted with a red disc that diminishes as the time elapses, giving a visual indication. (Sound can be added.) By telling the child, "We will go to the library when the red is all gone," you interrupt the stream of anxious questioning and give him a measure of independence in monitoring and managing his own time. For more information visit: http://www.timetimer.com/home.htm.

Choice is good. Those of us on the NT part of the world spectrum take for granted the amazing number of choices we have on a daily basis. Minute by minute we choose one option over others and know that both *having* choices and being *able* to choose provides us with a measure of control over our lives and our futures. The same cannot often be said for individuals on the autism spectrum. As a whole, their choices are much more limited, which can contribute to a lack of self-esteem, behavior problems and a reluctance to interface with the people and situations around them.

Providing frequent choices to children with ASD can have profound results: negative behaviors decrease, self-esteem and self-motivation grow and children become more actively engaged in everyday life.

- Give the child a choice rather than an imperative. Rather than saying: "Write your name and the date on the top of the page," say: "Would you like to write your name first, or would you like to write the date first?" or "Which would you like to write first, letters or numbers?" Follow with a visual cue: "See how Jason is writing his name on his paper?"

- When giving choices, whether written or concrete (objects), place the choices inside a circle. Verbal or written lists can be difficult for some ASD kids to process, hence they frequently end up merely choosing the last item offered or suggested.

- Whenever possible, offer a choice or a compromise within a "have-to." For instance, she needs to eat a piece of fruit with lunch; offer her a choice between a banana and an orange. No, he can't wear those muddy jeans to school today but you will run a special wash load later so he can wear them tomorrow.

- While giving your child a choice can have a positive impact on behavior, there will be times when offering a choice isn't realistic or safe. When this happens, avoid meltdowns by being clear and unapologetic:

    ~ "I can't give you a choice in this situation because it is dangerous. You might get hurt."

~ "I can't give you that choice because it would be bad for Danny" (have negative consequences for another child).

~ "I give you lots of choices but this time it needs to be an adult choice."

Give me a break! Provide a "quiet corner" or safe space where a student with ASD can go to self-regulate for a few minutes if he is feeling overwhelmed. The area can be as simple as a corner set apart by bookshelves facing in. Have a piece of carpet on the floor for sound absorption and tactile input, and provide a rocking chair or beanbag chair for proprioceptive/vestibular calming. Earmuffs, stocking caps or headphones may also help.

> *Tip:* Scheduling these short sensory-motor breaks into the child's day can be very effective in helping the child stay at optimal levels of attention and awareness, thereby improving his ability to get the most out of his day at school.

You gotta love where you work. Teachers, in order to help the child with autism you have to be taking care of yourself too. You "live" in your classroom as much as ten hours a day. Make it a place that you like and find little ways to provide yourself with calming, soothing or invigorating options. Do you like comfy sofas, pillows, soft lighting?

Program modifications. Many children with ASD can participate very successfully in general education classrooms when reasonable modifications to the curriculum or program are incorporated. Some of the more frequent modifications are listed below.

- Supplement verbal directions with visual cues and visual learning tools.
- Model the behavior or task to help her understand directions.
- Provide a quiet or "safe" place for him to go to recoup when overstimulated.

- Modify or shorten classroom work or homework.

  ~ Example: The fifth grade weekly spelling list is twenty-five words emphasizing the "un" prefix ("unreserved") and the "tion" suffix ("subscription"). Reduce his list to twelve to twenty words, and make sure he knows the root word ("reserve" or "subscribe") before adding the prefix or suffix.

  ~ Example: Modify math story problems for relevancy. If Billy doesn't play soccer and doesn't like chocolate, a story problem about selling candy bars for the soccer team has no relevance. Change the problem to helping Mom choose oranges and bananas at the grocery store, or separating his marble collection into colors and sizes.

- Make a keyboard (word processor, computer) available to facilitate written assignments if handwriting is cumbersome.

- Allow longer time for tests, or give tests in sections with a break or rest in between each section.

- Give tests in resource room or other less distracting but familiar environment.

- Verbally coach a child through tests, repeating directions between each section.

- Allow tests to be taken orally, with or without slight prompts ("What planet is closest to the sun? It starts with an M.")

Appropriate IEP goals. Whether it's a single teacher or several, the person providing instruction to a child with ASD is an invaluable team member in designing and implementing an education program that will reap benefits. While teachers may or may not be directly responsible for the educational objectives on a child's IEP, all teachers should check to make sure goals and objectives are meaningful to the child, measurable and quantifiable, and are aligned with the child's learning style.

Inadequately stated goal:
Chris will sight-read third-grade spelling words.

Defined, quantifiable goal:
Chris will sight read third-grade spelling words from
the Dolche World List both 1) in isolation and 2) in
context 225 out of 250 attempts, as reviewed quarterly
at the end of each grade period.

Inadequately stated goal:
Jordan will initiate play with a peer.

Defined, quantifiable goal:
Jordan will initiate play with a peer 1) with adult help
physically, 2) with adult verbal prompt, 3) independently, three out of four times on a daily basis, as record-
ed by staff observation with quarterly review and random probes.

Budding Michelangelos. Art can be a wonderful, expressive
medium for children with ASD, especially children who have limited-
to-no verbal communication abilities. The various mediums provide
sensory integration opportunities, especially tactile development,
while promoting fine motor control and hand-eye coordination.
Producing a visual, tangible product fosters self-esteem. Many individuals with autism are artistically gifted and make a living through art.

Teachers and parents can encourage children with autism to explore
their artistic potential in many different ways. Here are some useful
tips from an art therapist/paraeducator:

• Joint drawings can encourage a child to add detail they
might not otherwise think of on their own. The adult can
start the drawing—say, the house—then the child and adult
take turns adding details like windows, door, grass, flowers, a
weathervane, chimney, birds, the mailbox, clouds, a bike in
the driveway. Let it go on as long as the child maintains
interest. Then come back to it another day and add yet more
details. Pair verbal language with each detail as it's drawn;
practice spelling, pronouns or imagination. The educational
options are endless.

• Provide a model when the goal is to have the child draw
something specific. One art therapist says: "When a fabric
mural was being created with an artist-in-residence, my

student was to choose an animal to depict. It helped a bit to have a picture of the real animal he chose but still his drawing was not a recognizable ant. Then I drew the ant as he watched. I left him alone and he drew an ant that looked very much like mine—a believable ant."

- Step by step drawing is also helpful. This can be a whole class activity with the teacher leading.

- Art can segue into writing. Daily journal writing was painstaking for one little second-grade boy. Each day he would draw a train car with the single sentence, "My train is good." When pressed to write a second sentence, he would add something generic like "It is cool." His paraeducator noticed that while the writing was static, the drawings were taking on ever more detail: cars became either boxcars or flat cars with added features on the wheels, more cars were added to the train, people began appearing in them. The drawings continued to progress, even as the writing stayed stagnant—until the following year, when the floodgates opened and the child began writing a screenplay!

- Art can open the door to communication for children who are nonverbal or who cannot express their feelings otherwise. In one heartbreaking example, a paraeducator worked on a clay project for weeks with a nonverbal child. The school suspected child abuse, suspected the father, but couldn't prove anything. Week after week the child worked soundlessly away on a sculpture of a dark, gaunt figure. One day, the silence broke. He noticed another child watching him and said: "My mom is mean to me."

- Art can provide a visual medium for story creation. Children can be encouraged to create characters and several drawings depicting their characters in various situations. Concepts like sequencing and predicting can be taught using these visual representations.

Paraeducator-pro. Good paraeducators are worth their weight in gold; they facilitate increased opportunities for the student with autism to learn and grow. However, while most paraeducators are willing and eager to take on the duties they're hired to do, not all of them arrive to the classroom fully educated in autism spectrum disorders or teaching skills. It therefore is beneficial to all parties involved when the school administration takes steps to assure that the educational assistants they hire have the skills required to meet the child's needs.

- Start with a survey of needs that includes an assessment of the paraeducator's skills in relation to the duties of the position and the role s/he will take in the classroom. Is the paraeducator's knowledge of ASD sufficient to work with the student(s)? Is further education required in any areas?

- Conduct an initiation and orientation to the school. To whom does the paraeducator report—the teacher, the Autism Specialist, the school administrator?

- Discuss the school's policies, procedures, lines of authority and chain of command, dress codes, emergency procedures, etc.

- Review the class setting.

- Describe the tasks the paraeducator is expected to perform. Is he a one-to-one aide for a single student, or a teacher's assistant, too? Is clerical work expected? How is his/her time divided among responsibilities?

- Review a typical day's routine, preferably with input from the class teacher.

- Review the child's IEP and make sure the paraeducator understands the goals and objectives from a functional perspective.

- Review how best to get the child's attention.

- Review the child's reinforcer list.

- Make sure the paraeducator understands and can work with the child's primary communication system, especially with a nonverbal child (e.g., sign language, etc.).

- Discuss the child's social skills challenges so the paraeducator knows what to expect during interactions.

- Share the child's sensory sensitivities with the paraeducator and watch for new behavior issues that suddenly arise; they may have a basis in sensory issues (e.g., perfumes, grooming products, pet hair, etc.).

Peer power. Young children are naturally inquisitive and can be more than willing to help a student with ASD navigate her day, if they know a little about the disability and how best to interact with the peer. We asked several NT students who had friends with ASD for their best advice; here are some of their responses.

- Don't be afraid of them. Sometimes they act differently but they're still kids like the rest of us.

- Ask them to do things with you or a group. They know a lot of things and are interesting.

- If it looks like they don't know how to do something, show them what to do rather than telling them. It helps when they can imitate your actions.

- Offer to help when they look like they need it, but don't just do things for them. They have to learn just like the rest of us.

- Don't tease kids with autism. If you see someone else teasing them, tell them to stop.

- Make sure you get their attention when you want to tell them something. Otherwise, they might miss what you say.

- Treat them the same way you treat your other friends. They can be cool too.

- Sometimes they don't respond right away—they need more time to think about their answers. Be patient and don't rush them.

- Learn more about their autism, from their parents, or a teacher, or from the Internet. Ask about ways you can help.

- If you see them acting weird, remember that they can't help it. Sometimes their bodies act in funny ways because they're stressed out or anxious.

- Say something to them when they do good things. Give them a high-five, or just say "great job." They like compliments too.

- They have trouble with all the social stuff, so give them hints, or talk them through situations if you think it might help.

- A lot of kids with autism have sensory problems. They get stressed out in loud, noisy places where there's lots of people or things going on. If you see your friend getting agitated, suggest you both take a break for a few minutes and go someplace quieter.

Return address. Try having a child use dry-erase markers on a mirror to practice writing her name, address or phone number. It may add just enough interest to keep her going beyond her usual attention span. Or use the same technique for tic-tac-toe, spelling words or artwork. The markers clean up with glass cleaner.

Teacher for a day. If your child has one particular book he knows inside, outside and upside down, ask the teacher if he can "teach" it to the rest of the class or to a smaller reading group. He can lead the group in reading it, then ask questions that he has written down ahead of time (with the help of his teacher, therapist or parent) about the main characters, setting and sequence of events. Adapt questions as necessary for a nonfiction book.

> *Variation:* Ask if he can be a "guest speaker," visiting his former kindergarten classroom to read his favorite book to the "little kids."

Phonics hike. When the lesson plan involves learning new sounds for each letter of the alphabet, take a tour of the neighborhood or school grounds hunting up objects that start with that sound. Record the words in a journal or on a clipboard for the child or children: hallway, heat duct, Stony Hill School, history book, hoagie bun, hand dryer, door handle, door hinge, wall hanging, happy face sticker, hat, health room.

Variation: If you do the hike indoors one day, do it outdoors the next time. Children spend so much of their time indoors; take every opportunity to get them moving in the fresh air.

Language Yes/No game. This game encourages full-sentence responses, a requirement in many written school assignments. Give your child or student ten small items he likes—nickels, Tootsie Rolls®, marbles. He must answer all your questions that day without saying yes or no. Each time he doesn't, he gives you back one of the items. If you ask, "Did you turn in your spelling homework?" he cannot say merely "yes" or "no." He must say, "I put it in your homework box," or "It is still in my backpack." At first it might help to hold up the favorite item as a visual cue to remind him that a yes/no response will forfeit one item. Use your judgment and cut some slack while he adjusts to the game; frustration won't create learning. And make the game reciprocal. If you answer one of his questions with yes or no, you need to give him back one of his confiscated items.

Play to your child's interests. If your little collector owns enough Matchbox or Hot Wheels cars to simulate rush hour traffic (we know a child who did just that, every evening, down the main hallway of the house), be ever vigilant for ways to weave his interest into all areas of learning. Use those cars to:

- Combine tactile sensory with pretend play: Set up a shaving cream "snowstorm" and have him plow out stuck cars.
- Teach left from right or listening to directions by playing with the cars on a road-map children's rug or plastic floor map. "Go two blocks past the large tree and turn left."
- Make a memory game using a set of double prints taken of 24 of his favorite cars.
- Five red cars plus five blue cars = a custom tic-tac-toe game.

Take the stand. Make a "standing station" available in the classroom. This is a podium-like space where the child can go to work standing up if he needs a break from sitting. (Note: You may find your neuro-typical students asking to utilize this spot as well.)

Or the reverse may be true. Provide a mat or carpeted area where a child can read or do work lying down. Full-body contact with a firm surface may aid concentration.

Name that classmate. Your child's social interactions with his classmates may be complicated by the fact that he can't remember all their names. Ask the school to provide a class photo or photos of all the children, along with their names.

- Post the photo(s) on your refrigerator or bulletin board. Practice learning each child's name.

- After she has learned all her classmates' names, take it a step further. Talk about who has short blonde hair/who has long black hair. Oh look, he's wearing glasses; she has such a pretty smile.

- Then go another step further and talk about something the classmate is interested in: Carson loves to draw comics, Shawna plays the piano.

- Compare and contrast the children. Do any of them have the same name? How many of their names start with the letter K?

Task master. For the child who is prone to drifting off-task, place a photograph of him working on-task on his desk as a silent reminder. This can also help them keep their desk or locker organized. Post a picture of the tidy desk or locker before it hits cyclone stage. Keep in mind, however, that children must be taught how to use these cards. They cannot simply be posted in the room, in hopes the child will understand their purpose. Demonstrate their use and provide ample time for practice.

> *Variation:* Provide a photo for any school or home situation where a gentle reminder can be employed. Sitting properly in circle time, walking in line, putting lunch trash in the bin, where to hang up his coat are some

school applications. Setting the table, hanging up his towel, brushing his teeth, putting clothes in the laundry hamper are some home applications.

Note that this approach provides a concrete model that emphasizes positive behavior rather than criticizing improper behavior.

Sweet and sour. Pair a preference or preferred item with something he doesn't like to encourage less-than-desirable task completion. If she hates tooth-brushing, read her favorite story while she brushes, or play some favorite music. Let him chew gum while he picks up his toys or writes out his spelling words.

The Things to do Later bin. Interruptions are a fact of life. If a project or homework assignment needs to be interrupted (dentist appointment, dinner time, just plain fatigue), it goes into the Things to do Later bin—a specific place that visually reinforces that the child can or should return to it at a later time. For those days when planning runs amok, consider adding numbers to each item in the bin, to signify which one to do first, second, etc. Use sticky notes; don't write on the actual assignment.

Concept formation. The thinking pattern of most individuals with ASD is specific to general, as contrasted to neuro-typical thinking, which tends to be general to specific. This makes concept formation a difficult skill to acquire. It also partially explains the literal, black and white, rule-based way that most people on the spectrum relate to their world. Flexibility in thinking needs to be taught.

Promote concept formation by making a game of putting objects into new and different categories. Put a bunch of different objects on a table and start with simple sorting concepts: by color, by shape, by material or the letter of the alphabet the object's name starts with. As abilities develop, encourage the child to invent new categories. This step will be much more difficult and require assistance on your part. For instance: What can you do with a cup? You can drink from it, it can become a pencil holder, a vase for flowers, you can use it to measure out another substance, or more abstractly, as a paper weight, a plant holder or a door prop.

Make it fun. Lots of repetition is needed before the child learns to think differently. But results will occur.

Teach success. One of the simplest ways to build self-esteem in children is to incorporate an already mastered level of skill into a novel or difficult task. For instance, alternate new vocabulary words with mastered vocabulary words in a flash card drill. The idea can be incorporated into almost any teaching situation that takes place.

Visitors today. Teachers can set up a Visitor's Board with pictures of people who will be visiting the class that day. This will help your student handle changes in the schedule, surprises and fear of the unknown.

Integrated Play Groups. Young children with ASD may need assistance in developing play skills. Integrated Play Groups is a structured method of instruction that can do just that. Developed specifically for kids on the autism spectrum, it entails play groups composed of three to five children, with a greater number of typically developing children involved than children with autism. The play groups generally meet at regularly scheduled times at least twice a week for thirty to sixty minutes, in settings like integrated school sites, after-school programs, recreation centers, or homes.

The Play Group Guide—a teacher or sometimes a parent - guides the children through modeling and coaching, providing more support during the early stage of the group's formation than later. Initially the Play Group Guide may serve as a director, setting the stage for a performance—arranging play materials, assigning roles, setting up play events, and acting as an interpreter to help expert and novice players figure out each other's actions and words. At the next level the Play Group Guide moves closer to the periphery of the play activity, posing questions, commenting on activities, and offering suggestions, but always modifying his/her behavior in response to the patterns of activity in the play group.

The goals of Integrated Play Groups are many: to expand social awareness and interest in other children; to increase reciprocal social interaction and symbolic representation through cooperative pretend play; and to create genuine friendships either between children with autism and children without, or between two children with autism. The strategy was created by Pamela Wolfberg, who directs The Autism Institute on Peer Relations and Play. Learn more about it at www.autisminstitute.com.

Designed with Asperger's in mind. Just as not all children with classic autism will do well in a fully integrated setting, it is equally true that not all children with Asperger's Syndrome (AS) can learn and thrive in a mainstreamed classroom. While IQ levels may be high and language may be functional, the social and sensory challenges of AS students can interfere to the point that a different setting might be more appropriate. The school's special education class may not offer a student with AS the academic challenge he needs, nor the opportunities to learn from peers who exhibit socially appropriate behaviors. As more and more students are being diagnosed with AS, schools are finding that a workable option is to create a special education class designed specifically for the AS student. Characteristics of the class might include:

- About eight students and one teacher.
- Located in the regular school in a quiet part of the building.
- Same academic curriculum as regular education students.
- The room would be a sensory sensitive environment.
- Social skills training included as part of the curriculum: etiquette, friendship skills, body language, etc. Social activities included as 'homework'.
- Strong routine built into the daily schedule that includes private time for students.

- Alternative physical education options provided: miniature golf, shuffleboard, karate, dance.
- Curriculum modifications that would include extra practice on note-taking, task analysis, drawing conclusions, noticing implications, etc.

Color walk. Tie or tape a piece of solid-colored paper or tape around your child's wrist, then go for a walk around the house, the neighborhood or the mall looking for things that are that color. When she finds one, reinforce with language: You found a red book. You found a red jacket. You found a red wheelbarrow.

Could you re-phrase that? If you have given instructions several times and the child still cannot follow them, assume he does not understand. Are there too many steps? Are the instructions unclear?

- Try giving just one instruction at a time and then checking for comprehension.
- Don't keep repeating the same words over and over; instead, rephrase the instruction in a slightly different manner.
- Did you give him enough time to respond? Remember that he may have motor planning as well as language impairment and may need extra time to comply.

When, when, when? If a child in your class is asking repeatedly when the next activity will occur, place a card with a representation of a clock on her desk. The clock should look like the one in the classroom, with hands pointing to the appropriate time for the next activity. Go one step further and write "9:20 PE Gym" under the clock face; you will further reinforce time-telling skills as well.

This one's just right. One child may like the control and pressure needed to use colored pencils. Another child may prefer the ease of felt pens—instant color without needing to use pressure. Crayons may be more difficult; it is harder to control the edges, and pressure is needed to get good color. Paint is even harder to control, and has the additional complication of the "messy factor." Both art and writing projects have to be achievable AND make sense. The task may get done but with an obvious disconnection, ergo no benefit.

Beginning art for the photo-oriented child. For the child whose level of representation is at the photograph stage, illustrations and abstract art will not yet appeal. Begin introducing her to drawing by placing a clear laminate piece, taped in place, over a photograph and having her trace it, using a felt pen that wipes or washes off easily (like those intended for overhead projectors). This helps her learn about edges, shapes and concrete objects, and she can be successful with the finished tracing.

Easy adaptations for aspiring athletes. While team sports may present a difficult menu of challenges for some ASD kids, others naturally gravitate towards one type of team sport or another. Maybe it starts as a "special interest"; baseball players and stats are more interesting at first than actually playing the game. But somewhere along the way your son decides that being out on the field is something he really wants to do.

Adapted physical education specialists are teachers trained in making modifications to equipment and curriculum so that children with supplemental needs can participate in general education PE classes with their peers. PE can be a confusing mix of motor skills, rules and all the social complexity that goes along with the concept of teamwork and competition, offense and defense. However, being able to participate with peers goes a long way toward erasing yet another distinction that may separate the child with autism from his contemporaries.

Most of these adaptations are things you can also do at home to help your child become more skilled at common sports activities.

1. Vary the size of the equipment: a larger or smaller ball, a heavier or lighter bat, a larger racket head with a shorter handle, a golf club with a larger head.

2. Allow two hands for typically one-handed actions: dribbling the basketball, rolling the bowling ball, handling the tennis or racquetball racket.

3. Decrease distances: between bases, from the tee to the hole, from the mound to the plate. Stand closer to the net to serve; lower or eliminate the net. Stand several steps over the foul line at the alley. Adjust as skills increase.

4. Slow the pace of the activity down. Lengthen or shorten times as needed.

5. Provide oral or visual prompts or cues. Do not expect your child to remember rules if he is focusing on learning a motor skill. Visual aids are always a plus!

6. Speaking of rules, make sure you explain them to the child in a manner that he understands, even those that at first glance might seem obvious or simple. One child we encountered loved baseball, and was given a position in right field. When the ball came towards him, he didn't understand that he might need to run one way or another, forward or backwards, to catch it. He just stood there waiting for it to come exactly to his spot. Mom and Dad worked with him and at the next game he was back in right field. The very next hit headed midway between center and right field—a situation they had neglected to go over. Who runs for it? Team sports are highly complex. Even the most obvious rules, like running to the next base, usually involve many options.

7. Support from a peer partner or buddy may be more readily accepted than instruction from an adult. Choose a buddy whose skills are good but not so elevated as to make your child feel inadequate or discouraged.

8. Allow frequent rests if needed.

9. Use a tee for softball, baseball, tennis, golf.

10. Allow extra bounces in volleyball, tennis, racquetball, basketball.

11. Allow drop serves in racket sports.

12. Do the activity in an area with minimal external distractions.

13. Halt the activity if you sense your child's frustration building. Take a break or have the child engage in a calming activity and then try again or end the session and move onto something else.

14. Keep instructions short and clear. Do not use sports lingo unless you are sure the child understands the terminology.

15. Allow your child to choose an at-home activity: "I'd love to play with you after dinner. Shall we jump rope or toss the frisbee?"

16. Have the school's PE teacher and/or adapted PE teacher send you a weekly note or email regarding what the week's activities will be or have been. Reinforce at home, not just with the activity itself, but in talking about it, asking questions about it, reading or looking at books about it.

Reading suggestions:

Coach John and His Soccer Team, Alice Flanagan

Everyone Wins at T-Ball, Henry and Janet Grosshandler

My Basketball Book, Gail Gibbons

Children's Sports Movies:

Little Big League (baseball); *The Big Green* (soccer); *Little Giants* (football); *The Mighty Ducks* (hockey)

A tricycle by any other name. Three-year-old Michael's mom really wanted him to learn to ride a tricycle, but he was very afraid to take his feet off the ground ("gravitational insecurity" in OT terminology). His OT confirmed that he was very coordinated and there was no physical reason he couldn't do it. His teachers noticed that he always chose books about machines: tractors, cement mixers, combines, loaders. They began referring to the tricycle as a "machine," and having him acclimate to it gradually. First, he would just touch it. Then, sit on it briefly. It was a very short period of time before he was pedaling away. Sometimes just changing the name of the item is an inroad to interest and skill development.

Houston, we have no problem. Help your little spaceman or spacewoman transition to the next activity by "blasting off". Have him kneel, crouch or sit on the floor with you behind him. Start counting down: "T minus ten and counting—nine, eight, seven, six—we have ignition—five, four, three, two, one—we have liftoff!" Lift him off the floor and send him on his way to nap, bath, story time, chores or whatever his next activity will be.

The bridge to circle time. Teachers can help children switch from one activity to the next by using a physical task as a bridge. Inside of merely calling children to circle time, have them negotiate a physical task or obstacle to get there. It could be going up and down some low steps, crawling or wiggling under a table, following footprints or stepping stones/shapes, going under or over a limbo bar. This activity has the double benefit of providing calming input for the movement seekers and alerting the movement avoiders of impending input.

Acclimating to group work. If your student seems to work well one-on-one with a peer, give him as many opportunities as possible to do so. When he seems comfortable and confident, add a third person. Gradually increase the number in the group.

A Quick Reference Guide to successful inclusion. With appropriate supports and services, many children can be fully or partially included in regular education classes. Successful inclusion, however, requires attention to the environment, curriculum, teaching methodology and daily modes of interaction.

The following is a quick reference guide for teachers that outlines some of the salient points in making inclusion work for everyone in the class: the child, his peers and the teaching staff. Copy it, clip it and post it on your desk as a helpful visual reminder.

Teaching Methodology

- Use Visual tools:

    ~ A daily/weekly visual schedule; a monthly visual calendar

    ~ Visual cues during instruction

    ~ Posted classroom behaviors

    ~ Visual representation of time

- Discuss changes in the schedule ahead of time with the student; be specific.
- Teach flexibility and change as part of the normal routine.
- Make sure there is a clear end to each activity, and that it is reasonable for the time limit.
- Repetition, repetition, repetition: academic and social skills.
- Emphasize positive behaviors; tell the child what to do, rather than what not to do.
- Stay calm when behaviors escalate.
- Assess reinforcers regularly, at least once per month.
- Teach classmates an understanding of ASD and how to help the child with ASD.

Language/Communication

- Check for comprehension often: Beware of mere echolalic recitation.
- Supplement verbal instructions with written instructions; use pictures or words.
- Keep instructions simple and straightforward; avoid idioms, metaphors, figurative speech.
- Phrase requests in the positive.

Social skills

- Education is more than just academics; teach social skills.
- Model and role-play social situations incorporating appropriate behaviors.
- Provide social skills practice for any upcoming social events.
- Provide a social skills notebook with stories of correct and incorrect social behaviors.
- Discuss how others view his behavior and the social consequences of his behaviors.

Modifications

- Be sensory sensitive: sounds/smells/visuals/touch/motor.
- Provide a quiet place to work on assignments.
- Provide test accommodations: a silent room/extra time/alternative formats.
- Provide keyboard access rather than requiring handwriting.
- Provide a safe place the child can retreat to when needed.

Time's up. Some children with ASD will perseverate on objects or ideas or participate in other behaviors that can hinder academic progress during the school day. Trying to extinguish this type of behavior is not the answer; providing a time limit on such behaviors can help.

As soon as the child begins to exhibit an inappropriate, perseverative behavior, set the timer for a predetermined amount of time. The child is taught that as soon as the timer rings, she must rejoin the rest of the class in the current activity. As weeks go by, the time limit should be reduced so that less and less time is actually being spent on such inappropriate behaviors.

Summer's over: back to school strategies. Help prepare your son or daughter for the back-to-school transition by employing these ten ideas designed to ease them into the school routine again.

1. A few weeks before school starts, begin shifting bedtime to the school year routine; this helps get them used to morning routines again.

2. Simulate homework routines before the start of school. Have your child do quiet activities at a specific time and place every day. Guard against having your child perform preferred activities at this time; it's designed to set the stage for homework.

3. Review your child's preferred reinforcers and be creative about finding new ones if needed.

4. School clothes: If your child has to wear a uniform to school, wash it several times to "break it in." Have your child wear it for at least several hours prior to the first day of school to get used to it and determine if any sensory issues arise. Consider the same sensory issues with non-uniform clothing.

5. To help your child adjust to new people or new surroundings when transitioning to middle school, purchase a school yearbook. Then go over peoples' names and faces with the child before summer ends.

6. Videotape your child walking through the school schedule before school starts; let him review it often at home.

7. Practice routines, e.g., moving from class to class, going to lunch, recess, gym, etc.

8. Refresh your child's memory, if needed, with photos and names of people he will encounter on a daily basis: school personnel such as cafeteria workers, the school nurse, office staff, bus drivers.

9. Reacquaint your child with even familiar routines, like the route to walk to school, what time the bus leaves from school, how to get to the nurses' office, the library, etc.

10. Set up a few social gatherings, especially with a "peer buddy" before school starts. That positive social relationship set up ahead of time will be helpful in those early stress-filled days of school.

Oh, no, Mom! In our best-intentioned efforts to learn as much as we can about our child's day at school, many a parent will visit the school class, or cafeteria, unannounced to the child. Before you do, discuss your plan with the child, and ask his permission to be at school or join him for lunch. Some children with autism view a parent's lunchtime visit as an unacceptable breach of routine, and Mom's participation during class events as not-so-welcome interference. Respect your child's wishes. An interruption in routine that constitutes a violation of his need for order can color the entire remainder of the day in a very unhappy way.

I have a question. Wouldn't it be ironic if, in diligently teaching your child how to gain information through asking questions, you neglected to do so yourself—about the very school to which you are entrusting him each day? Moving to a new home is an obvious time to ask questions of school personnel. But even if you are not moving, you owe it to your child to ask the questions whose answers will determine whether he is going to be in an environment that encourages him to meet his full potential, or whether it's time to start shopping for an educational setting other than the neighborhood school.

- What is the school's overall culture in terms of dealing with bullying and teasing? Zero-tolerance is the only policy you should accept. If you hear a "kids will be kids, and we let them work it out themselves" approach, know that your child has neither the language nor the social skills to be able to hold his own in that atmosphere.

- What is the school's policy on parent visitation to the classroom? In these times, any school will require that you sign in and wear a name tag, but beyond that, are you welcome to drop in anytime? Can you visit with a day's notice? Or will you have to jump through hoops of fire to be able to observe your child's classroom? If your phone calls and emails are not returned reasonably promptly (within 24 hours), if the teacher has an endless stream of reasons why "that day wouldn't be good," if you get verbal agreement but the body language is telling you otherwise, speak to the principal at once.

• In what other ways are parents involved in the school? Are there parent representatives to site councils or advisory committees? Are parent development workshops offered through the school or the district?

• What is the average tenure of the general education teaching staff? What is the tenure of the special education staff? Low turnover generally indicates a positive working environment.

• Where is the resource room located? In the mainstream of the school, or tucked away in a little-seen corner?

• Does the district offer regular or ongoing in-service training, itinerant consulting or other professional support specific to autism for general education and special education teachers?

• How are IEP goals measured and quantified? IEP goals must be measurable and dictated by hard information collected in a clearly defined manner.

• Will the IEP be based on your child's actual needs or on resources projected to be available?

• What is the school or classroom culture regarding inclusion generally and autism specifically? A one-size-fits-all policy should raise your radar. Slotting your child into a special classroom without evaluating his individual needs is never appropriate.

• How will you be kept apprised of your child's progress? A communication book of some sort that travels back and forth from home to school each day is one way, a daily or weekly email or phone call is another. You should expect a written quarterly progress report for each IEP goal, but there must be communication in between or valuable time may be lost as problems fester.

All done. Many kids with autism get so fixated on a task (especially something they enjoy) that activities without a clear-cut ending can be anxiety-laden. Make sure your visual schedule has an "End of Task" square or a transition to the next activity square. When asking your child to help with raking the yard, define the physical area he is to complete (especially if it's a large yard). Not everything can be timed or physically portioned out, so make sure you're being concrete in other ways to help the child understand when the task is "done."

On the run. If your child or student is a "runner" (movement seeker/perpetual motion machine), he will dehydrate more quickly than his more sedate classmates. Allow trips to the drinking fountain as needed, or let him keep a water bottle on his desk. The water bottle may actually do double duty as an oral-motor calming device.

Walk a mile in these shoes. In the course of the twelve or so years of a child's school life, parents encounter teachers they love and teachers they could have done without (and teachers: we know the reverse is true). Some teachers seem to "fit" a child, his needs and learning style while others remain polar opposites, never achieving the reciprocal give-and-take that would facilitate learning. Yet, child and teacher and parent must still contend with each other over the course of the year, sometimes longer.

"Walk a mile in my shoes", "just spend a couple of days at our house"—such thoughts frequent the minds of parents in such predicaments. A few other thoughts that parents have shared with us, sentiments they wish that teachers would read and take to heart, follow. The life lesson here is not one of taking sides, or finding fault, but recognizing that each person experiences the world in a different way. For parents and teachers to effectively work as part of a team for the betterment of the child with ASD, it helps to periodically imagine life through one another's eyes.

• Please make no assumptions about what it is like to parent this student. He may exhibit an entirely different display of behaviors at home—for better or for worse. An open, non-judgmental and ongoing exchange of information between home and school is the only way for all concerned adults to get the complete picture they need in order to truly help the child.

• Because parents do know and experience the child in a manner and setting different from yours, respect what they know to be true about their child and accept their ideas and suggestions as tools, not criticism.

• Whether you think you can or whether you think you can't, "fix" or "cure" are words better left out of thoughts and discussions about your student with autism. By definition, autism is a spectrum disability and kids with autism will be as different as flakes of snow. No two are alike and their learning paths will differ. That requires accommodation and adaptation, but in any case, the child does not need "fixing." Suggesting that means the child is being seen as "less than"—and that attitude can only cause friction between parent and teacher. Work with parents to find the in-road to relevance for this particular child, and there you will find motivation, love of learning, the desire to improve and pride in accomplishment.

• Autism is an open-ended disability; there are no inherent upper limits on achievement. Expect more and you will get more. The hopes and dreams parents hold for their child help them maintain the stamina they need to stay the course long after their child has left your classroom. Respect and honor their dreams, and dream large for this student while he is in your class. Mom and Dad need to know that you, like they, are encouraging their child to be everything she can be.

• Respect and make use of the time and effort your student's parent has gone to in educating herself about the various aspects of her child's different ability. She has a need to know as much as she can about how her child sees the world, and much of what she has learned can make your job easier. It can also be comforting and sustaining for her to know that she is helping others, because . . . .

- Parenting the child with autism can be a lonely, exhausting experience on many levels. Offer positive reinforcement, encouragement, an ear or a shoulder when needed. And—judiciously—let her know that you have days like that too, so you can support each other's efforts.

- Believe that you can make a difference for this child. Most, if not all, professionals in the field of special education will tell you that children sense far more than they communicate. And the number one thing they sense is whether or not an adult believes that they "can do it." What are your visual and auditory clues telling the child? If you communicate an expectation that falls short of what he knows he is capable of, it is only logical that shut-off will follow. It's a trap. Don't fall for it. *Believe.*

Chapter 7

To Know the Law

Special Education Legal Strategies and Considerations

To know the law is not merely to understand the words, but as well their force and effect.

Justinian

Special education Cliff's Notes. Special Education law is a maze of new terminology, regulations and procedures that can boggle the mind of a parent whose child has recently been diagnosed with ASD. However, there are some basic and "big-ticket" parts of the law that parents should be aware of because they speak to the child's rights and govern the provision of services within the educational setting.

The Three Biggies. There are three major federal laws that govern the provision of special education services in the school system:

IDEA—the Individuals with Disabilities Education Act

Section 504 of the Rehabilitation Act

ADA—the Americans with Disabilities Act

In most instances involving children with ASD, parents will be obtaining services for their child under one of the first two laws.

FAPE (free, appropriate, public education) is what all students with disabilities are entitled to receive under federal law. FAPE refers to the quality of the education program that is provided to a child who is in need of supplemental instruction, and is further defined as 1) free—at no cost to the parents; 2) appropriate—designed and developed with that one specific child's needs in mind, which means that a one-size-fits-all program goes against FAPE; 3) public —to the maximum extent possible, the education is provided in the same public educational setting as the rest of the children who would normally be learning alongside that child had she or he not had a disability.

Least restrictive environment (LRE). LRE addresses where and how the child's services are to be provided. In a nutshell, it says that the regular classroom in your neighborhood, where a child's peers obtain their education, needs to be considered first before sending a child with autism into a more restrictive setting, e.g., a special education classroom or resource room, a different building, a different school. It's important to keep in mind that the full phrase used in the IDEA, a "free appropriate public education in the least restrictive environment" goes on to acknowledge that related services and supports are an integral part of this equation. The child is not to be thrown into a regular classroom without the necessary help he may need (a full- or part-time aide, modified curriculum, related services, etc.). Section 504 and the ADA have even more stringent requirements of schools: They must *demonstrate* that the student *cannot* be served appropriately in a regular educational setting, with the use of supplementary aids and services, *before* another setting can be discussed.

Related Aids and Services are intrinsically important for children with ASD who manifest the sensory, communication, and social skills challenges inherent in the disorder. They are defined at 20 U.S.C. 1402 (22) as "such developmental, corrective and other supportive services as may be required to assist a child with a disability to benefit from special education." The Supreme Court also defined them as: services that enable a handicapped child to reach, enter, remain at school during the day and exit. We're not just talking academics here. Related services can refer to anything that helps the child get to school, stay at school, learn the curriculum, participate in the extracurricular activities afforded to her NT peers, and return home at the end of the day. The code, at 34 C.F.R. 300.24, provides a list of fifteen related aids and services; this list is by no means exhaustive of what can be provided for your child. It is within this part of the law that help with social skills, sensory issues, language/communication, play skills, leisure/recreation skills and more can all be addressed.

Prior Written Notice is required whenever the school district wants to change *anything* in regard to the child's educational program or related services, whether the request comes from the school or the parent. For instance, the school wants to drop the one-to-one aide from the classroom, or thinks that a child's level of OT services should be increased or diminished. A parent asks the school for additional speech therapy. The written notice also extends to those times when the school refuses to initiate or change the student's program as a result of a parent request.

The precise wording of the notice is in 20 U.S.C. 1415(c). The most important aspect of Prior Written Notice of which parents and teachers should be aware is how Congress defined the **content** of the notice. It was designed to be thorough, so that each action taken with regard to a child's educational program was well thought out and addressed with care. Prior Written Notice, by law, must contain the following:

- A description of the action proposed or refused by the school.

- An explanation of why the school proposed or refused to take that action.

- A description of any other options that the school considered and the reasons why each of those other options were rejected.

- A description of each evaluation procedure, test, record, or report the school used as a basis for their proposed or refused action.

- A description of any other factors that are relevant to the school's proposed or refused action.

Transition planning is required under the IDEA, Section 504 and the ADA. Planning is to begin "when determined appropriate for the individual, beginning at age fourteen or younger" and the plan must include, at the minimum: Transition Services, Rehabilitation Counseling, Assistive Technology Services, Recreation Therapy and Social Work Services.

The purpose of transition planning is to prepare the student for independent living, access to employment, access to further education and training, and access to recreation and leisure activities in the community. Section 504 is very strong on the point that the programs or services selected for a child—*even a child in the earliest years of elementary school*—should be preparing him for these transitions once he graduates from high school. As you're working out goals and objectives for a child with ASD of any age, keep in mind those overarching, life-affirming goals of graduation, moving on to further education if desired, having a job and living independently in the community. They should be guiding decisions as the educational plan is developed.

Extended school year (ESY) refers to services provided over the summer months to keep a student from losing the gains she made during the regular school year. Extended school day services also falls within this realm of additional services. Both speak to the provision of services to help a student maintain his level of academic or functional ability while school is not in session. ESY services can be difficult to obtain in some school districts, and although regression is not required to be demonstrated first in order for a child to be eligible for services, in reality that is often the case before schools will acknowledge the need and work with parents on providing a program through all or part of the summer break.

Know how to register a formal complaint. At some point or another, parents and their school system will butt heads over an issue and be unable to smoothly resolve an issue. While a Due Process Hearing (i.e., going to court) is an available legal remedy to parents, these authors suggest that Due Process should be only initiated as a last resort, after all other remedies have been exhausted unsuccessfully.

A more effective remedy for parents is to become knowledgeable about and utilize the formal complaint process included within the law. The U.S. Supreme Court described the steps needed to make a successful complaint to a school district in Gebser v. Lago Vista Independent School Dist., 524 U.S. 274 (1998) and again in Davis v. Monroe County Bd. Of Ed., U.S. 629 (1999). Parents who follow these steps usually end up resolving their issues with the school—successfully—without needing to go to a Due Process Hearing.

Start a Special Education binder, in which you place copies of correspondence with the schools, your child's records, etc. A chronological format works well; it gives you history and allows you to see how far you've come with securing appropriate services for your child. It may or may not be necessary to say, but we'll say it anyway: *Put everything in writing.* Document conversations you have with the school as to the provision of services, requests you make, etc. These will not only help refresh your memory as time passes, they will provide you with a paper trail should you run into an impass with the school at some point in the future that requires legal action.

Where to find the law. Free copies of the three federal laws-IDEA, Section 504, and ADA, can be found on the Internet at various special education websites, such as those offered by Reed Martin, J.D. (www.reedmartin.com), Peter and Pamela Wright (www.wrightslaw.com) or the U.S. Office of Special Education (www.ed.gov/about/offices/list/osers/osep/index.html).

The following references may help:

- Statutes are the actual laws passed by Congress, and are in the U.S. Code (USC): the IDEA is at 20 U.S.C. 1401; Section 504 is at 29 U.S.C. 794; and the ADA is at 42 U.S.C. 12131. The Family Educational Rights and Privacy Act (FERPA), which governs parents' access to their child's records, is at 20 U.S.C. 1232g.

- Regulations (the "regs" as you'll hear them called) are written to implement each of these statutes. Regulations serve as "instructions" that explain exactly how a statute should work, and specifically what must be done. They are published in the Code of Federal Regulations (CFR). The IDEA regulations are at 34 C.F.R. 300., Section 504 is at 34 C.F.R. 104., the ADA is at 28 C.F.R. 35 and FERPA is at 34 C.F.R. 99.

Be sure to ask. If you don't understand something being discussed at an IEP meeting, be sure to speak up and ask for an explanation. School personnel often use obscure acronyms and terminology, or refer to test scores and assessment results in odd jargon; it can be confusing, or new, to even a seasoned parent. Ask questions whenever you're not 100% sure of information being discussed.

The negotiator. Hopefully, you and your school have an amicable relationship, and are working together as a team to create an appropriate educational program for your child. That doesn't mean you will always agree on every point. Keep in mind that obtaining services for your child is a *negotiation*. Know when to press a point and when to back off, and give a little. Be clear about where you can bend and where you want to stand firm, before you enter the meeting. Expect to offer compromise in order to reach some common ground that is acceptable to both you and the school.

Helping hands. Because the special education laws are so complex, parents (and teachers) won't be able to synthesize everything there is to know initially. As time passes, new issues will come to the forefront and require additional reading and attention. That's okay; don't beat yourself when you encounter something unfamiliar. But do become educated about it, at least at a basic level, so you can interact intelligently within your team and know the parent/school rights in the matter. In the meantime, these ideas may help:

- Parents can tape record the IEP meeting; it gives you the opportunity to focus on the discussion at hand without the added stress of taking notes or documenting what was agreed upon. Plus, it's useful to refer back to the discussion once the meeting is over to make sure everything said was heard.

- Parents can bring another person with them to the IEP meeting to take notes, be there for support, or to advocate on their behalf for educational services.

- Most schools prepare a preliminary IEP before the actual meeting, as a starting point for discussion. Parents can, and should, request a written copy of the document prior to the meeting, that includes all relevant reports, assessments, evaluations, etc., that the school used in generating their recommended program and services. It provides time to read the document at a slower pace, assimilate all the information and come to the meeting prepared with intelligent questions and comments.

- Parent support organizations exist in every state and provide a range of services, from training workshops on special education issues to providing advocates to accompany parents into IEP meetings. PTIs (Parent Training Information Centers) are organizations that provide parents with advocacy, training, and information on their children's educational rights; P&As (Protection and Advocacy) agencies are federally mandated in each state and territory and provide protection of the rights of persons with disabilities through legally based advocacy. Find referrals in your state at the Resource section of the Autism Society of America's website, www.autism-society.org.

Contact your school district's special education department to find out if there is an IEP Partners program or similar support available. IEP partners are familiar with the special education system, help parents plan for the IEP meeting, coach them on effective presentation of their concerns, attend the meeting with the parents, provide follow-up to the meeting and direct parents to additional information and resources.

Equal partners. In creating the federal laws, Congress was adamant that parents should be equal partners in deciding what programs and services are to be provided for children with disabilities. References to parent participation are frequent throughout both the IDEA and Section 504.

However, it can be easy, in the middle of all the PhDs, Ed.Ds, M.A.s, or PsyD-credentialed people who may be part of the IEP team for a mom or dad to feel, well, a bit intimidated. Don't. With regard to the student about whom the meeting is taking place, the mom or dad is the individual who best knows that child, who has spent thousands of hours observing, working with, listening to and learning about the child, from his conception to the day of the meeting. Parents may not know all the jargon and legalities of special education, but they do know their child. Their knowledge is priceless.

We agree to disagree. It's three hours into the IEP meeting and the end is in sight. The discussion has been contentious and the parent is not all that pleased about many of the items included on the IEP document before her. At the end of any IEP meeting, parents have the following options:

- Sign the document, which will be interpreted as their consent to the provision of services outlined in it, unless indicated otherwise;
- Sign the document indicating partial consent to services specified as such, and disagreement with services specified as such. In this case the school can proceed with the services agreed upon.
- Remind the school district, in a very short note on the IEP minutes, that the school has refused some of the parents' requests, and ask that "Prior Written Notice" be sent to the parents.

A relatively easy way for parents to voice their objections to either the procedures taken by the school in conducting the meeting, or the content of the IEP document itself, is to take into the IEP meeting their own form, which they fill out as the meeting progresses. Parents then direct the school to add a copy of the form to the IEP materials to more clearly reflect the parents' position. The "IEP" is the written product of the meeting—it is not limited to just the document that the school district brings into the room.

The annual IEP meeting is held to plan a year's worth of services in the life of a child—*your* child, not the school's child. Therefore, parents should object to anything that lessens their ability to participate in the IEP meeting, to influence what is written down on the IEP, or that isn't appropriate and individualized for the child.

Creating positive partnerships. Strong, effective partnerships are usually based on a few general principles: honesty, respect, empathy, commonly shared goals and commonly shared ideals. The relationship between parents and schools is ideally a solid partnership, with all participants working effectively for the benefit of the child with ASD. However, at times the emotional nature of the issues being discussed can disrupt even the best-intentioned participants. To follow are tips for parents and school staff in creating positive partnerships.

- Acknowledge that you are part of a team, with a common goal of creating the best possible educational program for the student with ASD. Resolving issues in a win-win format is essential to fostering a long-term positive relationship. Leave egos and attitudes at the door.

- Read the IDEA, Section 504, the ADA and familiarize yourself with the rights of parents and the responsibilities of the school system with regard to the provision of services. Don't leave it up to someone else. Be personally educated and responsible.

- Be respectful of those present: present your opinions firmly, but politely. Avoid putting team members on the spot or consciously embarrassing them.

- Explain concerns clearly, without unnecessary jargon. Present specific examples; be able to back up your statements with facts. Check for comprehension often.

- Arrive on time, organized and prepared. Have questions ready.

- Keep a check on your emotions: Learn how to discuss, disagree and reason with others to accomplish your goals.

- Base decisions on the child's need, not in response to the personalities or interpersonal skills of team members.

- Accept that a team member may have a differing point of view, but still hold the child's best interests in mind. No one is always right or always wrong.

- Establish a rapport and maintain communication throughout the year. Share information freely. Return calls promptly, write notes often.

- Express appreciation for the things that deserve appreciation —even the little things.

Additional thoughts just for parents:

- Keep in mind it's not about YOU. You're there to advocate for your child and create the best possible educational intervention plan possible.

- Respect that teachers and administrators are responsible for the educational program of many other children besides your own. They may not always be able to respond to your requests immediately.

- Be realistic about what constitutes a crisis and what is a concern. Only call an "emergency IEP meeting" when necessary.

- If you decide that due process is warranted, say so honestly. Using it as a threat or as blackmail is unprofessional and will only breed distrust.

Additional thoughts just for school personnel:

- Know that "district policy" or state law does not override federal law. Don't be afraid to say so when you see a discrepancy.

- Recognize the parent as the expert in understanding the child and how he functions.

- Don't be embarrassed to seek advice from other professionals, or request further evaluations in areas of need or uncertainty.

- Understand the gravity of the decisions that are being made about this one child. They will affect their success or failure not just this year, but in the future as well.

Appropriately trained staff. Parents now have a right under the No Child Left Behind Act to write their school, and ask for a response in writing, about the credentials, qualifications and training of personnel who are going to be in contact with their children. What is their autism experience and training? If you feel that a staff member doesn't understand your child's condition and could benefit from more formal autism training, or the educational program set up for your child is not incurring benefit, ask about the specific autism training of the people involved. It may be time for a refresher course, an in-service workshop or the help of an outside autism specialist.

Good faith effort. Across the U.S. today, school systems are increasingly aware of the positive results that can be obtained with students with ASD when appropriate education and services are provided. Wonderful teachers accomplish wonderful results with students with ASD. Supportive administrators make sure their staff keep up-to-date with emerging thought, receive training on the latest therapies and services, and provide quality education to the children in their systems. Unfortunately, the opposite is also true, perhaps even more so. Teachers are ill-equipped to have a child with ASD in their class, administrators deny needed services for all sorts of reasons, and school systems spend more money in legal fees fighting parents than the requested services would have cost.

Law makers have taken an increasingly strong stance in the last few years that supports the idea that providing appropriately trained staff is *not enough* in designing a child's education plan. The IDEA at 34 C.F.R. 300.342(b)(3) speaks to everyone involved with a student's IEP being informed and responsible, and requires that a school district assure that:

"Each teacher and provider is informed of his or her specific responsibilities related to implementing the child's IEP and the specific accommodations, modifications, and supports that must be provided for the child in accordance with the IEP."

The IDEA carries it one step further, to accountability, requiring that school personnel involved make "a good faith effort to assist the child to achieve the goals and objectives or benchmarks listed in the IEP." Congress upped the ante for schools—making them not only responsible, but accountable—in response to their audits that discovered that not a single state in the U.S. had fully complied with federal requirements for the provision of special education services.

View this as a wake-up call: Recent changes through Supreme Court decisions (see Gerber v. Lago Vista and Davis v. Monroe) provide the possibility that not just the school, but that school staff, *individually*, can be named in a lawsuit a parent initiates against the school.

Sent home, once again. Autism is a behaviorally based disorder, meaning the social, communication, cognitive or sensory deficits manifest themselves in overt behavior. That's precisely why the interventions and treatment programs within autism target appropriate behaviors as an end result. Most parents and teachers by now understand that behavior is communication, especially on the part of ASD children. They recognize that the behavior is not willful, but is a manifestation of the challenges the child is working to address. Schools know that when challenging behaviors erupt that interfere with the ability of the child to benefit from education, or that compromise the ability of students around the child to learn and grow, the IDEA requires that a very sophisticated and comprehensive evaluation be undertaken to determine the source of the problem, the conditions under which the behavior manifests and then to design a Positive Behavior Intervention Strategy and Support Plan. Some schools even know that the evaluation has to be done within ten days of the acknowledgement of the behavior problem, and comply.

The reality of what parents encounter is often a different story. When the child's behavior is too much for the teacher(s) to handle, the often-employed strategy is to suspend the child, often repeatedly, with no further action on the part of the school to investigate why the behavior is occurring or to incorporate a new behavior plan and/or modify the child's educational program. Depending on the severity of the behavior problem, some kids with ASD are expelled, spending months out of the school year at home, without benefit of education.

Schools may feign ignorance of their responsibilities to evaluate and handle behavior issues, but they are responsible nonetheless. What can parents do? Send a letter to the school, describing the behavioral issue in writing. Ask for a behavioral evaluation, and once obtained, a new IEP meeting. If the school still stalls, send another letter requesting Prior Written Notice from the school, where they are required to explain their refusal to conduct the evaluation and the meeting to develop the Positive Behavior Intervention Strategies and Support plan. That should get their attention.

Mediation alert! Numerous meetings have been held, you brought along an advocate and still you and your school system cannot agree on the aspects of the educational plan for your child. To resolve the issue, the school may suggest formal mediation. Sounds good, but beware.

The benefits of mediation are many: it occurs at no cost to the parent, there's generally a very short resolution time period compared to the months or years that could be involved in a Due Process Hearing, and parents could walk away at the end of a proper mediation with a 'done deal', as opposed to a hearing, where the losing party can appeal into court and keep the process going.

But there's also a downside that is often not explained to parents— a serious one. Parents who voluntarily enter into mediation and then go on to accept a written agreement as a result of the mediation, waive rights to ALL claims made to the school up to and including the date of the signed document, *whether or not they were addressed in the agreement.*

While mediation can sometimes be a useful tool in obtaining needed services, parents should be aware of what they give up when accepting an agreement through mediation. Generally, it will benefit parents more to refuse mediation when offered and pursue other grievance mechanisms first (the GEBSER format for a written complaint under the IDEA.)

Regular teachers' rights in Special Education.

Teachers are the mainstay of education. As more and more students with disabilities are being fully or partially included in regular classrooms, it behooves regular education teachers to not only know about the educational rights of students who need supplemental services, but to also familiarize themselves with their own rights in providing educational instruction.

Recent changes in special education law that hold not only administration staff, but also teachers personally liable for lack of a "good faith effort" in providing the needed educational services make it imperative that regular education teachers not only know their rights, but can exercise them freely for the benefit of each and every child they teach.

- **Right of teachers to participate in a self-evaluation of the school district.**

    The self-evaluation examines the policies, practices and procedures relating to students with disabilities and provides an opportunity for teachers to raise questions as interested parties, and receive answers that address their concerns.

- **Right to seek assistance for a student in a classroom who is not receiving benefit.**

    The program for a child with ASD in a class just isn't working. Teachers have a right—and a responsibility—

to make a referral or request an evaluation where assistance is needed.

- **Right to act as a child advocate.**

    The ADA recognizes teachers as advocates, and outlaws retaliation, intimidation or reprisals for teachers who advocate for children.

- **Right to have the child fully evaluated.**

    The child has a right to be evaluated in every area that might adversely affect educational performance. This is not limited to academics, but includes speech/language, sensory issues, social skills development, leisure and recreation, play skills, daily living skills and a host of other areas.

- **Right to receive any training needed under the Comprehensive System for Personnel Development.**

    If the key to serving the student appropriately is teacher training, then the teacher has a right to receive that training.

- **Right to participate in the IEP process that develops the plan for a student in their class.**

    The statute includes "the child's teacher" as a participant in the IEP meeting. All questions a classroom teacher might have regarding curriculum modifications, methods of teaching, positive behavior supports and systems, delivery of services, etc. must be asked and answered before the child comes into the classroom.

- **Right to receive the related services that should honestly be on the IEP.**

    If services are agreed upon at the IEP, but are not provided in the classroom, it violates the teacher's, student's and parents' rights. Remember, as a teacher you are not only responsible, but *accountable*, for the delivery of services that will confer benefit to the child.

- **Right to be recognized as an advocate for all the children in the classroom.**

  A classroom teacher has a duty to all the children in the classroom—those with disabilities and those without. Congress is adamant on placing children in the least restrictive environment possible, recognizing that the interests of typical children, and the ability of the teacher to teach the classroom, need to be balanced with the right of a child with special needs to be in that regular classroom.

- **Right to participate in assessing the effectiveness of the program.**

  Once the IEP is implemented the teacher must have a role in assessing whether the IEP is working, and if it is not, reconvening the IEP team to make appropriate modifications.

- **Right to be treated as a professional.**

  Teachers are not just subordinate employees expected to carry out orders without questions. They are educated professionals with, in most cases, a sincere desire for all students to learn and excel.

It is clear from legislative history that Congress viewed the teacher as an important participant in the delivery of special education services—just as important as the parent or the school administrator. When regular education teachers learn and live by the rights afforded them, ALL children they teach can learn and grow to their full potential.

Endnotes

From Chapter 2—The Limits of My World

Beware of idioms in your speech. Instructions for the Go Fish Idioms Game were adapted from http://www.glc.k12.ga.us

Visual strategies. "How to create a visual schedule" was adapted from information appearing on Linda Hodgdon's website, www.UseVisualStrategies.com.

Jump starting literacy for concrete thinkers. Adapted from the article "Real Animals Don't Talk: Nurturing a Book Lover When Fantasy Isn't Part of Their Reality" by Ellen Notbohm; *Autism Asperger's Digest*, March-April 2004.

From Chapter 3—Strong Reasons

When stubborn behaviors persist. Adapted from the article, "10 Everyday Teaching Bloopers & How to Avoid Them" by David Freschi that appeared in his Simply Good Ideas column; *Autism Asperger's Digest*, March-April 2004.

Deals and Contracts. Adapted from the article, "Deals and Contracts" by David Freschi that appeared in his Simply Good Ideas column; *Autism Asperger's Digest*, September-October 2003.

From bad to worse: how to avoid escalating a skirmish. Adapted from L. Albert's *A teacher's guide to cooperative discipline: How to manage your classroom and promote self-esteem*, 1989.

From Chapter 4—To Do and Understand

Just Take a Bite. Adapted from information presented by Dr. Ernsperger in a workshop (Utica, NY 2004) and also contained in her book *Just Take a Bite: Easy, Effective Answers to Food Aversions and Eating Challenges* by Lori Ernsperger, Ph.D. and

Tania Stegen-Hanson, OTR/L. 2004. Future Horizons, Inc., Arlington, TX. www.FutureHorizons-Autism.com

Uncommon gifts for uncommon kids. Adapted from the article, "Uncommon Gifts for Uncommon Kids" by Ellen Notbohm that appeared in her Postcards from the Road Less Traveled column; *Autism Asperger's Digest,* November-December 2004.

Staying dry at night. Adapted from information presented in the book, *Toileting Training for Individuals with Autism & Related Disorders* by Maria Wheeler, 1998. Future Horizons, Inc., Arlington, TX. www.FutureHorizons-Autism.com

Home safety for escape artists and acrobats. Ideas were adapted from information offered on the Special Needs Children's Network website, http://archive.specialneedschildrennetwork.com/archive/sncn2.html

Medications: be sure to be thorough. Adapted from the article "Medications and Informed Consent" by Luke Tsai, M.D. that appeared in the Ask the Experts column; *Autism Asperger's Digest,* January-February 2002.

From Chapter 5—A Sensitive Awareness of Others

Friend to friend. Adapted from information offered on the Friend 2 Friend Social Learning Society website, www.friend2friendsociety.org.

From Chapter 6—Learners and Doers

Designed with Asperger's in mind. Adapted from the article, "Is There a Continuum of Alternative Placements for Students with Asperger Syndrome?" by Gretchen Mertz; *Autism Asperger's Digest,* July-August 2004.

The driver on the bus says . . . . Adapted from the article, "Tips for Riding the Bus" by David Freschi that appeared in his

Simply Good Ideas column; *Autism Asperger's Digest*, November-December 2003.

From Chapter 7—To Know the Law

Special education Cliff's Notes. Adapted from the article "The 'Special' Language of Special Education Law" by Reed Martin that appeared in his Special Education Law column; *Autism Asperger's Digest*, January-February 2002.

Creating positive partnerships. Adapted from the article, "Creating A Positive Partnership Between Families and School" that appeared in the *PDD Network* newsletter, June 2002.

Regular teachers' rights in Special Education. Adapted from the article "Regular teachers' rights in Special Education" by Reed Martin that appeared in his Special Education Law column; *Autism Asperger's Digest*, March-April 2004.

Index

S

T

V

W

About the Authors

Author, consultant and parent of a child with autism, **Ellen Notbohm** is chief executive and founder of Third Variation Strategies LLC in Portland, Oregon. A columnist for *Autism Asperger's Digest,* her articles on autism have appeared in *Exceptional Parent, South Florida Parenting, Children's Voice* and other magazines. Beyond autism, her published works encompass a diverse range of local and national newspapers including the Chicago Tribune, genealogical journals, baseball magazines and family publications. She holds a degree in Speech Communication from Southern Oregon University.

Veronica Zysk has been working in the field of autism since 1991. She served as Executive Director of the Autism Society of America from 1991-1996, and then joined Future Horizons as Vice President of Administration. Veronica moved into an editorial position within the company in 1999, as Managing Editor of the first national magazine on ASD, the *Autism Asperger's Digest*. She continues today as editor of the *Digest* and also provides editorial and consulting services within the autism community.

Printed in the United States
108612LV00008B/1-108/A